Swift's Narrative Satires

ALSO BY EVERETT ZIMMERMAN
Defoe and the Novel

Swift's Narrative Satires

AUTHOR AND AUTHORITY

Everett Zimmerman

Cornell University Press

ITHACA AND LONDON

First published 1983 by Cornell University Press.
Published in the United Kingdom by Cornell University Press, Ltd., London.

International Standard Book Number 0-8014-1595-0
Library of Congress Catalog Card Number 83-45176
PRINTED IN THE UNITED STATES OF AMERICA
Librarians: Library of Congress cataloging information
appears on the last page of the book.

The paper in this book is acid-free and meets the guidelines
for permanence and durability of the Committee on Production
Guidelines for Book Longevity of the Council on Library Resources.

Contents

Acknowledgments

This book has benefited from the assistance of more people than I can acknowledge specifically. Many—but not all—of my debts to other scholars are explained in the notes. Several people read earlier drafts of the manuscript and made helpful suggestions: Laura Brown, Sharon Cameron, Robert Hume, and Muriel Zimmerman, among others.

During various stages in the preparation of the manuscript, I have had research and clerical assistance from a number of people, including Jody Millward, Jeanette Hawley Smith, Rhoda Stewart, Leslie Cheek, and Kristina Nash. Some of this assistance was supported by grants from the Academic Senate Committee on Research of the University of California, Santa Barbara. I have also benefited from the resources of the library of the University of California, Santa Barbara, and the William Andrews Clark Memorial Library, Los Angeles.

Among the many students who listened with welcome enthusiasm or salving forbearance as I worked out early versions of the ideas in this book, I particularly acknowledge Mark Ferrer, Christopher Lauer, Judith Messick, and Timothy O'Brien, each of whom is now in one sense or another my colleague. I am grateful to my senior colleague William Frost, whose assumption of my administrative duties in the fall of 1980 enabled me to complete the penultimate draft of this book.

The Prose Works of Jonathan Swift, Herbert Davis, editor, is

Acknowledgments

quoted by permission of Basil Blackwell, Publisher. *A Tale of a Tub,* edited by A. C. Guthkelch and D. Nichol Smith (2d edition, 1958), © Oxford University Press 1958, is quoted by permission of Oxford University Press.

EVERETT ZIMMERMAN

Santa Barbara, California

Swift's Narrative Satires

Introduction

The revolution in epistemology of the seventeenth and eighteenth centuries made the relationship of the perceiving subject and the perceived object a centrally important one. This relationship, notably analyzed in Locke's *Essay Concerning Human Understanding*, had of course long been of philosophical importance, but it achieved an unusual force in conjunction with the development of the new science, the alterations of political and religious forms in England as a result of the two seventeenth-century parliamentary revolutions, and the changes in the literature of the eighteenth century.

Considered broadly, the relationship of the perceiving subject and the perceived object is a pervasive theme of world literature; in the new fiction of the eighteenth century, however, it occupies a prominent position formally as well as thematically. One notable strand in the novel which develops from Defoe through Richardson to Sterne is an epistemological and hermeneutical skepticism. In the major fictions of these writers a perspective less limited than that of its central character, its narrator-author, is posited, yet the precise limits and distortions of this character's perspective are not defined. Indeed in Sterne's *Tristram Shandy*, narrative, which ostensibly orders and clarifies, is itself a source of the confusions in which its narrator-author is mired.

Satire is seemingly a very different thing; it defines and corrects the moral and intellectual perspectives of fallen man by measuring them against the laws of nature and God. Rather than succumbing to the limits of human understanding, it defines them. A somewhat more uncertain version of satire nevertheless develops in Swift's long narratives, *A Tale of a Tub* and *Travels into Several Remote Nations of the World*. As the narrative extends, its narrator becomes increasingly an object of attention. The narration becomes an index of the narrator's relationship to a world as well as a measure of that world's shortcomings. Like *Tristram Shandy* (for which Swift's *Tale* is a source), Swift's satires exploit the potentialities in narrative for distortion as well as for order. The argument in my book is not, however, designed to redraw the generic lines of novel and satire but to explore the strategic position of Swift's satires in relation to major developments in intellectual history and narrative.

A Tale of a Tub and the *Travels into Several Remote Nations of the World* dramatize a putative author who shapes the narrative materials of his text, thus locating within these satires an analogy to the external relation of author to text. These works emphasize the literariness of satire. They show a satiric text coming into being because of the choices of its putative author, and consequently they challenge satire's conventional claim that it iterates objective truths.

The status of the narrator has been a persistent question in studies of Swift's satires. Answers have ranged from Maynard Mack's argument that all good satires create a persona, a narrator who must be differentiated from the biographical author, to Irvin Ehrenpreis's view that "*A Modest Proposal* makes sense only if we treat the voice as the author's throughout," a view that he extends to other satires.[1] The assumption in this book is

---

[1] Maynard Mack, "The Muse of Satire," *Yale Review* 41 (1951–52), 80–92; Irvin Ehrenpreis, "Personae," in *Restoration and Eighteenth-Century Literature: Essays in Honor of Alan Dugald McKillop*, ed. Carroll Camden (Chicago: University of Chicago Press, 1963), 35. Robert C. Elliott, "Swift's 'I,'" *Yale Review* 62 (1973), 372–91, summarizes and clarifies the issues of the controversy: "In any event it is certain that our author's voice is heard throughout. The question is whether the voice should be heard as issuing directly from Swift's own mouth or through the mediation of spokesmen he has invented" (p. 378). C. J. Rawson, *Gulliver and the Gentle Reader: Studies in Swift and Our Time* (London: Routledge and Kegan Paul, 1973), discusses the difficulties of

that the question of the narrator's status is closely related to the larger hermeneutical and epistemological issues in Swift's satires; it is not a narrowly rhetorical concern that must be disposed of as quickly as possible in order to arrive expeditiously at Swift's opinions. To accept an a priori categorization of Swift's narrator is to dissolve one of the important issues that Swift asks us to contemplate.

The "author" within the text is not easily relegated to a uniform rhetorical function: both tale-teller and Gulliver are skillful satirists as well as patently self-aggrandizing authors. Consequently these narrators do not have a simply defined rhetorical relationship to their creator, Swift. Instead of allowing the reader to assume the existence of an authoritative author from whom the satire emanates, Swift requires the reader to search for the principle of authority that validates the satire.

Several related contexts are relevant to Swift's consideration of this question of the author's authority: Protestant biblical hermeneutics, the epistemology of empiricism and the new science, and the political struggles of seventeenth-century England. A concern with valid authority is manifested in each of these areas, as each is an expression of individualism and provokes a countering concern for a principle of authority to subdue the resulting subjectivism. Protestant biblical hermeneutics is explicitly the concern of the allegory in *A Tale of a Tub*, and the issues of biblical hermeneutics enter the secular aspects of the *Tale* when its putative author urges the reader to interpret the digressions allegorically and typologically. The *Travels into Several Remote Nations of the World* too explores an area of secular hermeneutics that is rooted in biblical interpretation: the relationship of the literal to the allegorical. These categories were once a province of biblical hermeneutics, but by Swift's time they were also subject to pronouncements by exponents of the new science. Exemplifying the Royal Society's program for the

---

separating the real from the putative author in Swift. Rawson chooses to emphasize the "central Swiftian personality" which, "behind the screen of indirections, ironies, and putative authors . . ., is always actively present, and makes itself felt" (p. 6). I am concerned with the meaning of Swift's putting difficulties in our way as we attempt to understand his position.

advancement of scientific knowledge (travel reports were one aspect of that program), Gulliver suppresses the obviously allegorical (and even allusive) tendencies of his narrative in the interest of truth, which he believes is expressible only as the literal and univocal. The Puritan upheaval of seventeenth-century England is also allied to a hermeneutic program, an individualistic one entailing consequences that from Swift's perspective led to a usurpation of political authority. Swift urges that in these several areas a seemingly public and objective claim of authority is often grounded in a private desire for advancement. His encapsulating fiction for expressing this view is the figure of the "author" who claims the authority of truth for the vehicle of his self-aggrandizement.

Swift's critique of the intellectual movements of his time is conducted through his transmutations of inherited literary forms, a comment on the connections of the literary to the intellectual situation. Swift uses and analyzes literary forms bequeathed to him by such writers as Erasmus, Montaigne, and More, relating them to more recent events and intellectual developments. Swift's satires are often excluded from discussions of the development of narrative; nevertheless, at a time of significant changes in narrative method (near the birth of a new kind of fiction subsequently called the novel), they explore the orientation that became commonplace in later fiction: all is mediated, no perspective is final, and fiction is not identical to the world it purports to mirror. Swift's major satires analyze the context in which the novel arose, engaging the hermeneutical and epistemological concerns that are implicit in the new form. The present volume is concerned generally with Swift's analysis of a context that produced and included, among many other analogous developments, the novel. This book assumes generic impurity, however, and it is not particularly concerned with the degree to which Swift's narrators are "characters," according to one or another specialized definition. Nor is it concerned with documenting Swift's influence. Ronald Paulson has already traced the process by which the novel absorbed satiric fictions.[2]

[2]Ronald Paulson, *Satire and the Novel in Eighteenth-Century England* (New Haven: Yale University Press, 1967).

Northrop Frye describes three phases of language, the third of which designates the phase that includes the novel: the metaphoric, in which an identity between man and nature is assumed; the metonymic, in which the terms of one level of reality are used to stand for another reality; and the descriptive, in which the criterion of truth is the correspondence of language to something external and verifiable. According to Frye, this third phase of language "accompanies certain tendencies in the Renaissance and Reformation, and attains cultural ascendancy in the eighteenth [century]. In English literature it begins theoretically with Francis Bacon, and effectively with Locke. Here we start with a clear separation of subject and object, in which the subject exposes itself, in sense experience, to the impact of an objective world."[3] The "clear separation of subject and object" and the consequent concern with verifiability generate the "formal realism" that Ian Watt sees as characteristic of the novel.[4] The novel is concerned both to authenticate itself, by claiming reference to externally verifiable details and events, and to concede (and often to emphasize) the limitations of any subject's view. In *A Tale of a Tub* and *Travels into Several Remote Nations of the World,* Swift analyzes that sharp separation of object from subject and the limits of the rationalism or materialism that result from accepting either as the sole criterion of truth. He reveals the implications of the view of language, reality, and the subject's relationship to both that was becoming commonplace in his time. As all of Swift's readers know, his satires have a nearly irresistible force of their own; they also repay study in their context because of Swift's always intelligent, if sometimes unfair, analysis of a historical moment, aspects of which continue to impinge on us.

Chapter 1 of this book, "The Authority of Satire," introduces the contexts in which Swift's works will be considered, especially the conventions of narrative and satire, the developments of Protestant biblical hermeneutics, and the new science. The successive chapters fall into two parts: Chapters 2 through

[3]Northrop Frye, *The Great Code: The Bible and Literature* (New York: Harcourt Brace Jovanovich, 1982), 13.
[4]Ian Watt, *The Rise of the Novel* (Berkeley: University of California Press, 1956), chap. 1.

4 deal with *A Tale of a Tub*, and Chapters 5 through 7 deal with the *Travels into Several Remote Nations of the World*. Each of these parts explores a related set of issues: the narrator's use of a body of intellectual materials to create a relationship of self to world; the narrator's transformation of a literary form or forms to represent self; the epistemological implications of these processes. The literary forms and the bodies of intellectual materials used by the narrators differ in the *Tale* and in the *Travels*, as does the process by which the self absorbs and is structured by the narrative. Together the two satires represent Swift's analysis of the limits of human understanding and the uses of literary fictions to avoid acknowledging those limits.

The Authority of Satire

Narrative tends to represent itself as a version of the flux of life, always including too much to be intelligible without some systematic reduction. Even the parables of the New Testament are often not convincingly circumscribed by their apparent point: "A narrative of some length, like the Good Samaritan, works hard to make the answer obvious and in so doing provides a lot of information which seems too important to be discarded, once the easy act of completion is performed."[1] Historians too find that narrative, itself an interpretation of prior events, is not easily subdued to its intended analytical meaning: "The historian must 'interpret' his data by excluding certain facts as irrelevant to his narrative purpose. On the other hand, in his efforts to reconstruct 'what happened' in any given period of history, the historian inevitably must include in his narrative an account of some event for which the facts that would permit a plausible explanation of its occurrence are lacking."[2] Literature, Northrop Frye suggests, exhibits a tension between linear movement and "the integrity. . .of completed form."[3] Linear movement is narrative, and formal integrity is

[1] Frank Kermode, *The Genesis of Secrecy: On the Interpretation of Narrative* (Cambridge: Harvard University Press, 1979), 24-25.
[2] Hayden White, "Interpretation in History," in *Tropics of Discourse: Essays in Cultural Criticism* (Baltimore: Johns Hopkins University Press, 1978), 51.
[3] Northrop Frye, "The Archetypes of Literature," in *Fables of Identity: Studies in Poetic Mythology* (New York: Harcourt, Brace and World, 1963), 14.

meaning. Formal integrity is, however, sometimes defined only in relation to an extrinsic interpretive theory, which is granted authority by a privileged institution. Furthermore, like history, some works of literature claim a relationship to an external reality or system that does not adequately subsume their narrative aspects.

In allegory, for example, an opposition of narrative to meaning is sometimes apparent. The narrative is, on occasion, presented as yielding to a meaning rather than being identical to it, needing a figure like Interpreter in *The Pilgrim's Progress* or a book like the Bible to control the narrative. Satire has an obvious affinity to allegory, although only some satires are accepted as allegorical. Both presume that reader and author share a context that remains incompletely represented in the narrative. Consequently, the interpretive model provided by allegory—the narrative read as if it were an oblique version of a prior book, scheme of thought, or historical situation—is widely accepted as appropriate to satire.[4] Satire thus shares allegory's difficult relationships to narrative. Satire aims to confine the apparent fluctuations of narrative within an evaluative framework. The genre invites us to share the godlike vision of the satirist, in which our usual imperceptiveness is regarded as symptomatic of our debased condition. Satire is static and conceptual; narrative is a process and evades conceptualization.

Satire often uses allegory to reveal the gap between earthly process and moral imperative. The allegorical as a creative, or interpretive, strategy is conveniently adaptable to the metaphysical view that the secular and the sacred, body and spirit, are intimately connected. But allegory alternatively implies

[4]Ellen Douglas Leyburn, *Satiric Allegory: Mirror of Man* (New Haven: Yale University Press, 1956), discusses the close relationship between satire and allegory: "Critics write as if there were something incongruous in the two. How foreign this impression of incongruity was to ancient rhetoricians is indicated by Quintilian's including irony and mockery, which we link with satire, under the kinds of allegory" (p. 8). Gay Clifford, *The Transformations of Allegory* (London: Routledge and Kegan Paul, 1974), finds Swift to be "a crucial transitional figure in the development of allegory" (p. 111) and argues that "works of an allegorical nature from the late seventeenth century onwards...are conceived in a spirit hostile (sometimes violently so) to any attempted systematization of life" (p. 110).

18

that the physical is only an appearance beyond which lies a spiritual reality. These differing uses of allegory can be seen if we compare *The Divine Comedy* to *The Pilgrim's Progress:* Dante emphasizes the connections of the sacred to the secular, Bunyan their opposition. Narrative is allied to the secular and the literal—the world treated as independent—while allegory implies the incompleteness and disorder of narrative and of the world that narrative reflects. It is exaggerated but not entirely wrong to regard our assumption of an affinity between the terms "literal," "realism," "narrative," and "novel" as a reflection of the triumph of secularism. As the novel becomes the dominant narrative form, its claim of literalism is thought to give it a validity that allegory lacks.

Swift's major satires, *A Tale of a Tub* and *Travels into Several Remote Nations of the World,* make the oppositions of the literal and the allegoric, and of narrative and satire, into both formal and thematic concerns. The tale-teller divides his work into narrative segments and digressive commentary, losing both narrative continuity and satiric focus. Eventually he questions even the premises of satire, having eroded the moral framework by which he distinguishes what we praise from what we abominate. Gulliver imposes a travel narrative on his satire, implying that satire is embedded in the very movement of existence. But his generic distinctions become risible as his narrative encapsulates materials that are not assimilable to travel literature.

Swift satirizes the interpretive procedures of both of his narrators. In the *Tale,* he puts in narrative form a satirical account of the history of biblical interpretation in which the dominating issue is the relationship of the literal to the allegorical. He replicates the distinction between the two in formal aspects of the *Tale* and the *Travels,* in one of which the narrator embraces the allegorical, in the other the literal. *A Tale of a Tub* is heavily metaphoric and allusive, the *Travels into Several Remote Nations of the World* resolutely literal and spare. Both the dogged secularization in the *Travels* and the frenetic attempts at spiritualization in the *Tale* represent the self-serving choices of their putative authors, who illustrate the unstable elements in the Protestantism of Swift's time. Swift creates a vision that reveals the limits of these styles. While providing a critique of the metaphysical underpinnings of the secular literalism that Ian Watt and others have regarded as exemplified in the new fiction of the eighteenth century, Swift's satires also expose the allegorizers as obscurantists who act from self-interest.

Swift's *Tale of a Tub* reflects both the changing biblical interpretation of the Reformation[5] and the implications of biblical criticism for the interpretation of secular works. In the brothers' manipulations of the will, Swift parodies both the allegorization characteristic of Roman Catholic biblical interpretation and the literalism characteristic of Protestant, especially Puritan, interpretation. Furthermore, he extends the specifically religious issues of the *Tale* to more general questions about writers and readers, about allegory and allegoresis. As Maureen Quilligan remarks, Swift is concerned with "the dangerous tendencies of readers, particularly 'modern' readers, to become more powerful than their texts."[6] In addition, Swift explores the authority of writer over reader, in which lies the possibility of a demagoguery that exceeds the restraints of a text and of the world external to the text but putatively reflected in it. The *Tale*'s narrator adapts the methods of biblical exegesis to the production of meanings that exalt the writer: his description of "Oratorial Receptacles or Machines, contains a great Mystery, being a Type, a Sign, an Emblem, a Shadow, a

[5]Jay Arnold Levine, "The Design of *A Tale of a Tub* (With a Digression on a Mad Modern Critic)," *ELH: A Journal of English Literary History* 33 (1966), 198–227, discusses the relationship of Swift's *Tale* to issues of biblical interpretation in the seventeenth century. He argues that the putative author of the *Tale* is primarily a critic of Scripture: "The abuses in learning and the abuses in religion, then, are not only merged in Swift's basic design, but in fact emanate from one source, the egomania of the modern sacred critic, for whom the Bible is one more text to be trod upon in his assertion of self" (p. 206). Paul J. Korshin, "Swift and Typological Narrative in *A Tale of a Tub*," *Harvard English Studies* 1 (1970), 67–91, discusses "Swift's use of Biblical typology for satiric purposes in *A Tale of a Tub*, principally in Section VII, 'A Digression in Praise of Digression' " (p. 67). Korshin finds that the narrator's "devious misapplications of typological method . . . associate him closely with the undercurrents of Puritan dissent" (p. 91).
[6]Maureen Quilligan, *The Language of Allegory: Defining the Genre* (Ithaca: Cornell University Press, 1979), 141.

Symbol, bearing Analogy to the spacious Commonwealth of
Writers, and to those Methods by which they must exalt themselves to a certain Eminency above the Inferiour World."[7]
When Swift erupts into the controversies of biblical interpretation in the crucial period of the late seventeenth and early
eighteenth centuries, he focuses on the demand for private authority that characterizes authors and interpreters alike. The
three brothers' operations upon the Will are governed by their
own wills, and the narrator demands that his text too be interpreted in accord with his desires for acclaim.

In adopting an allegorical form for his *Tale* in a time when allegory was vanishing, Swift emphasizes the questions of interpretation and authorial authority that result from the shift in
the religious and epistemological situations of his time. Maureen Quilligan argues that "allegory always presupposes at
least a potential sacralizing power in language, and it is possible to write and read allegory intelligently only in those cultural
contexts which grant to language a significance beyond that be-
longing to a merely arbitrary system of signs."[8] Writing in a
context in which language is increasingly granted only the
power to represent the private vision of its user, Swift measures
the implicit claims of allegory against the explicit desires of his
putative author. The narrator of the *Tale* claims a sacralizing
power for his language but exposes his entirely secular aims as
he does so. In Protestant literalism, the incarnate Word, God
in history, was used to retain both letter and spirit within the
language of Scripture. But in a world in which writing reveals a
private vision and interpretation another, perhaps incongru-
ent, one, the Word becomes words. Appropriately enough, after the failure of the Puritan revolution and during the rise of
empiricism, Swift uses an allegorical form to scrutinize inspiration and interpretation in relation to both sacred and secular
texts.

[7]*A Tale of a Tub*, ed. A. C. Guthkelch and D. Nichol Smith, 2d ed. (Oxford:
Clarendon Press, 1958), 61. All subsequent references to the *Tale* are to this
edition.
[8]Quilligan, *The Language of Allegory*, 156.

21

The narrator of the *Tale* accords his work scriptural status, hoping to be translated by "the most Reverend Fathers, the *Eastern* Missionaries" (p. 106). The reader is encouraged both to interpret the *Tale* and to see it, like Scripture, as a compendium of interpretations of all thought and history. The narrator connects his work to biblical exegesis and to the interpretive tradition in which classical texts are allegorized to expose the true meaning hidden in an ostensibly different story. The work contains "Innuendo's" for the benefit of the commentators who must illuminate its dark points (p. 186), and it attempts to draw other works into its own compass: for example, the *Tale* completes Homer, having "exhausted all that the Human Imagination can *Rise* or *Fall* to" (p. 129). The various systems from which the tale-teller derives his authority, however, are blatantly arbitrary. Although he claims to absorb all history into his text, he obliterates history: "But I here think fit to lay hold on that great and honourable Privilege of being the *Last Writer;* I claim an absolute Authority in Right, as the *freshest Modern,* which gives me a Despotick Power over all Authors before me" (p. 130). His modernist claim substitutes the author for history.

The *Travels into Several Remote Nations of the World* appears to be a very different kind of book. Gulliver resolutely avoids both the allegorization and the figural claims that are characteristic of the tale-teller. The narration of the *Travels* is determinedly flat, avoiding historical and literary analogies even when they seem obvious. The tale-teller takes every opportunity, even a pun, to imply that his work has some deeper, or higher, or broader, or just "other," meaning than is apparent. But when, in one of his very few acknowledged allusions to other writers, Gulliver quotes Virgil to defend his own veracity, he writes with no suggestion that he knows the context that gives Sinon's speech a meaning differing from the literal.[9]

[9] *The Prose Works of Jonathan Swift*, ed. Herbert Davis (Oxford: Basil Blackwell, 1935–68), II:292. *A Tale of a Tub* is cited in the Guthkelch and Smith edition, but all other references to Swift are to the Davis edition. Volume and page number will be cited in the text.

A Tale of a Tub parodies the text that accretes authority from a prior text, the *Travels* the text that acquires authority from its literal rendering of nature. The *Tale* mimes an attempt to subsume all other claims to authority, the *Travels* an attempt to supplant all other claims to authority. These sharply dissimilar procedures have a similar aim—authority and autonomy for the narrator. The tale-teller makes his book so indiscriminately suggestive that he seems to be attempting to imply in figure and allegory all other thought. Gulliver makes his book so singular that he seems to be claiming all its implications as his own. He suppresses the suggestiveness of his story, making it his unique experience. In one case, the inclusiveness of the story gives its author final literary authority. In the other case, exclusivity achieves the same end. Both Gulliver and the tale-teller exert a "Despotick Power over all Authors before" (*Tale*, p. 130). Gulliver, like the tale-teller, attributes a scriptural authority to his book. Not only does he insist on the absoluteness of the truth of his book, but he believes that his vision of the goodness embodied in the Houyhnhnms would have put a stop "to all Abuses and Corruptions" if the English Yahoos had not been incorrigible (9:6).

Allegory relies on some prior condition, conceptualization or, often, book for its authority. But instead of giving the source outside the text, the pre-text, a privileged position (for example, as *The Pilgrim's Progress* is related to the Bible), satire demeans it.[10] When related to a privileged pre-text, allegory acquires an authority external to its author, but when the pre-text is suppressed or demeaned, this authority is weakened, making us rely on the author. Instead of suppressing this sense of diminished authority in a satirical allegory, Swift emphasizes it. One method of acquiring authority for the author of a narrative is to consolidate the forces of author and narrator, having the narrator display a wisdom within the narrative that reflects his creator's wisdom. Another method is to set author and nar-

---

[10]Quilligan, *The Language of Allegory*, 192, separates the satires of Swift and Pope from proper allegories on the basis of this changed relationship to a pre-text.

rator against each other, the obvious failures of the narrator pointing to the author's superiority. In the first of these methods the narrator becomes part of a personal allegory as the author's representative; in the second, the narrator represents some evil within a historical allegory. But Swift's narrators are only with difficulty relegated to either function. Instead, they resist identification with the author by usurping his role. Both the tale-teller and Gulliver are satirists who are aware of the evils that are represented in their narratives. And both explicitly display themselves as authors and discuss questions of their craft. Their self-display is bumptious and aggressive, however, not a sober display of authorial responsibility. Instead of being a conduit for Swift, these narrators make it difficult to apprehend him.

The distinction may be made more apparent by means of a comparison to *The Drapier's Letters*. The drapier is biographically distinguished from Swift, but he controls the ironies of the letters, and he shows his awareness of the evils that he describes rather than his implication in, or obfuscation of, them. Although he represents only one version of Swift's view, he is used as a particularly apt explicator of the dangers of Wood's halfpence and not as an oblique example of a complex evil that he does not acknowledge. This interpretive model will work only imperfectly for the *Travels*. Gulliver is indeed an apt viewpoint from which to observe the satiric scene. As a character, he undergoes experiences that convince him that humans are justly an object of satire. He also interacts with that scene, sometimes becoming an exemplar of evils that he describes. Still, we need posit no great separation between Gulliver and Swift as long as the failures of the character are marked, even implicitly, by the narrator: noting the failures of a life, especially our own, is a way of showing our perspicuity as well as our continuity with the flawed life. But the attempt to reduce the dissonance between Gulliver and Swift is sabotaged by Gulliver's explicit manipulation of generic conventions. Gulliver aggressively and unbelievably defines his book's origin as bare truth unaccommodated to the conventions of fiction. He suppresses his book's obvious similarities to a multitude of other familiar works, insisting that it embodies only the eyewitness veracity characteristic of the best travel literature. Gulliver's ruminations on the appropriate genre for the *Travels,* and his invidious comparisons of lying books to his truthful one, are not just the conventional claims of satire to truth. While attempting to establish his literal perspective, Gulliver calls attention to his literary ambitions and his shaping imagination rather than to his veracity. He attempts to place his reader at the appropriate vantage not only for understanding the experiences recorded in the book but also for understanding the achievements of Gulliver as author.

Questions of genre inevitably raise questions of authorial stance, putative or real. Genre suggests both a certain kind of event and a shaping of the event to fit a conventional literary pattern. In satire the event is often pitted against its literary shaping, as when in mock epic an inappropriately small event is shaped according to the patterns conventionally used for epic events. But whether the result is a satire or an incompetent imitation depends on the reader's hypothesis about authorial stance: "As Virgil is said to have read *Ennius,* out of his Dunghill to Draw Gold; so may our Author read Shakespear, Milton, and Dryden, for the contrary End, to bury their Gold in his own Dunghill."[11] When the author implied by the work is aware of the demeaning effects of an incongruous juxtaposition of form and content, we have a satire either of the content or of the form—satiric parody. If the parody is unmarked by an external perspective, however, we have a difficult problem of interpretation. Hugh Kenner makes the interesting observation that "To Augustus" is just the kind of poem an inept poet (Ambrose Philips, for example), might have written. It becomes a satire when Pope signs it, identifying himself as the obviously knowing creator of an inept work.[12]

Swift complicates rather than simplifies this interpretive problem by dramatizing his narrators themselves as ambitious

[11]Alexander Pope, *The Art of Sinking in Poetry,* ed. Edna Leake Steeves (New York: King's Crown Press, 1952), 39.
[12]Hugh Kenner, *The Counterfeiters: An Historical Comedy* (Bloomington: Indiana University Press, 1968), 92–93.

authors who are also perceptive satirists. The narrator-author of the *Tale,* for example, is both aware of human weakness and perversely willful. Like Gulliver, he organizes a satiric commentary, and also, by means of his generic choices and manipulations, exhibits his own shaping imagination. His expressed intent is to narrate a story of three brothers, obviously a historical allegory, but eventually the allegory is absorbed by his mock encomium of the moderns, and the mock encomium itself becomes a praise of the fool who narrates it. The form that makes the greatest claim to objectivity—the historical allegory—is absorbed by the self who narrates. The tale-teller's exhibition of the craft of his work—his division of it into instruction and delight—finally leads to an attempted display of tale-telling without a tale. Generic choices here, and in the *Travels,* are dramatized not as inevitable results of the historical or putatively historical content of the narration but as the narrator's way of making use of his story.

The explicit introduction of authorial choices and rationalizations into the texts implies that the satirical allegory is to some degree the creation of the narrator and, consequently, is symptomatic of him. The narrator as author is not, then, simply one among other satiric targets, for example, a figure who sometimes conducts Swift's attack against dissenters and at other times exemplifies the modern authors whom Swift despises. While the satire may be grasped as a series of local effects independent of any comprehensive form, such a reading is unsatisfactory, given the presence of an author-narrator whose literary shapings are made so apparent. The narrator's depiction as author gives him a priority over other objects of the satire.

Swift's image of the modern author as a combination of blindness and insight depicts the possibilities for understanding at a moment in history when absolute truths are asserted but the basis for man's appreciation of them has been undermined. Nature and Scripture remain values for Swift, but he is intensely aware that man's understanding of both is the product of a private mind with solipsistic proclivities. Consequently any conception of nature figuring its own meanings is compromised. The authorial dilemma that Swift dramatizes became conventional in later fiction: no perspective is total, all is interpreted, and the shape of literature is not congruent with that of life. Swift shows his narrative coming into being because of a particular perspective, not because it has an objective, uninterpreted existence.

But placed against this dramatized subjectivity is the implication of satiric allegory that its norms are impersonal. In satire the narrative is itself presumed to imply a normative shape. These satires, with their emphasis on their creators, call into question the very possibility of satire. Without at least the pretense that it represents a preexistent situation, the work loses any polemical import.[13] Satire ought, in a loose sense, to be emblematic or figural: it assumes a meaning in things themselves or in history itself. Its fictions imply that its words are connected to things that figure their own meanings.

The reader's position in relation to an authorial position as ambiguous as that represented in Swift's works is difficult. Swift appears in the interstices between the putative author's meaning and the meaning that is assumed to be inherent in the narrative events. The incongruities within the work imply that an author controls the limited narrator, but the incongruities are not thereby resolved. In a sense, the reader's control of the work partakes of the same arbitrary nature as the narrator's. The reader's vantage is his or her own interpretation of the narrator's tale. Readers may choose to subordinate the narrator to the historical allegory or the historical allegory to the nar-

---

[13]Edward W. Rosenheim, *Swift and the Satirist's Art* (Chicago: University of Chicago Press, 1963), 31, defines satire as "an attack by means of a manifest fiction upon discernible historic particulars." He notes that satire is distinct from art "which is purely rhetorical" (p. 23), because satire has a fiction that is a recognized departure from literal truth (pp. 17–18). Some version of the definition formulated by Rosenheim is assumed in most discussions of satire, although the arguments of Alvin Kernan, *The Cankered Muse: Satire of the English Renaissance* (New Haven: Yale University Press, 1959), chap. 1, against the emphasis on satire's affinities with polemical writing have also exerted much influence. John R. Clark, in *Form and Frenzy in Swift's "Tale of a Tub"* (Ithaca: Cornell University Press, 1970), has argued vigorously in his introduction and in chap. 1 that the *Tale* is a work of "mimetic art," not only a polemical work (p. 3).

rator, because Swift rules out neither approach. Swift is there as the figure we may use to lend authority to either interpretive mode.[14] Indeed, a history of the exegesis of Swift's satires might divide his commentators into those who emphasize the narrative aspects of his works and those who emphasize the satiric allegory. Commentators on narrative are concerned with narrators, process, continuity; their opponents accuse them of turning satires into novels. People concerned with satiric allegory tend to focus on image and referentiality; their interest lies in the confining of history within a conceptualized moral scheme that fixes process in the summary judgment. Their opponents accuse them of reducing narrative to polemic, of discarding the richness of means that is inapplicable to their neat summations of end.

Swift exposes the literariness of satire, just as Lucian exposes Homeric epic. For Swift, satire is not a privileged form, and its author is not exempted from explicit scrutiny. Satire conventionally winks at those of its implications that do not facilitate its polemical intents. And readers blink at those aspects of satire that do not fit the polemical intent preordained by the author's biography and expository writing. Still, Swift's satires demand of us the difficult process of searching for an authoritative perspective rather than just assuming Swift's perspective.

Swift articulates a crux that occurs in the interpretation of art and nature when the relationship between words and things is perceived to be unstable. St. Thomas Aquinas's view of the relationship between words and things implies that words designate things and that the things designated by the words have their own meanings. Meaning is increased without becoming contradictory. But the new science suppresses the emblematization of nature, substituting a science of primary qualities. Dealing with the gap between the differing meanings of word

[14]Robert W. Uphaus, *The Impossible Observer: Reason and the Reader in Eighteenth-Century Prose* (Lexington: University Press of Kentucky, 1979), suggests that "many eighteenth-century texts do not reinforce the expectations of 'objective' criticism so much as they challenge the reader into a new or renewed awareness of just how problematical the nature and formation of all beliefs, assumptions, expectations, and value judgments are" (p. 2).

and thing, the Royal Society attempts to bridge it, to make the word signify a true conceptualization of a thing. This use of language is an attempt to evade the apparent truth that the words represent only the private understanding of their user. An experiment described properly ought to have its benefits conveyed with universal success. Both Aquinas and the Royal Society attempt to give to language an authority beyond the intention of its author: it represents more, or perhaps less in the case of the Royal Society, than an author's meanings. Because the gap between thing and word, or conception and word, does not quite vanish, however, there remains unacknowledged personal allegory—a private meaning always intervenes between word and thing. In tracing the consequences of the new scientific view in the later eighteenth century, Earl Wasserman remarks that the older relationship of physical, moral, and spiritual is reduced to a relationship between the material world and qualities of mind: "Correspondences had become a phase of psychology, not ontology."[15] Swift's narrative satires articulate this process of verbal and ontological change.

Satire's customary attack on other literature is its way of obliterating the gap between word and thing. Satire defines itself as nonliterature, making its words represent the filthy things themselves and its judgments those of nature. But as Alvin Kernan has argued, the dynamics of satire tend to draw satirists into their scene, making them at one with the things they satirize.[16] Swift's narrative satires are extreme versions of this centripetal force. In Swift, in fact, the satirist threatens to absorb the scene. Revealing their fictive manipulations, Swift's narrators expose satire as literature, as an author's product, not the world's.

There is finally no conflict between the polemical purposes and the literary forms of Swift's narrative satires. Swift's most inclusive polemical purpose is to allow no privileged human perspective. This purpose is consonant with his politics. His

[15]Earl Wasserman, "Nature Moralized: The Divine Analogy in the Eighteenth Century," *ELH: A Journal of English Literary History* 20 (1953), 68.
[16]Kernan, *The Cankered Muse*, chap. i.

objection to Hobbes's politics is that Hobbes lodged in a single ruler the power that should be given to an elected legislature.[17] And Swift recognized that such a legislature too might make laws that contradict the very nature of things. With all his Hobbesian assumptions about human propensities for civil disorder, Swift was, nevertheless, not about to accept the Hobbesian solution for the conflicts engendered by human subjectivity—endowing with absolute authority another equally fallible human.

The key theorist who attempts to reconcile human and divine authority is in Swift's time still Richard Hooker, whose argument (one closely related to that of St. Thomas Aquinas) is that reason and revelation are both authoritative. People are governed by Scripture and also by natural law, which is derived from God and is manifested in his creation. Consequently a human society may make laws that, in reflecting natural law, are also in accord with God's laws. Hooker views the seeming oppositions of the secular and the sacred as complementary, capable finally of being reconciled in a society with a united church and state, neither having to be subordinated to the other. This vision of society is based on a belief in the universality of reason. Conferred by God, reason allows people to organize a secular society that is in harmony with God's order.

Still, changes in the seventeenth-century conception of reason undermined Hooker's views. According to Peter Munz's analysis, Hooker's reason is "the same [as] it had been to the Middle Ages and to Antiquity; it implied an intuitive as well as a discursive element."[18] But the term narrowed during the seventeenth century, becoming especially relevant to the inductive

[17]Swift, *The Sentiments of a Church of England Man*, in *Prose Works*, ed. Davis, 2:16. In this same work, Swift defines a position similar to Hooker's on the relations of church and state. Swift rejects the dissenters' attempts to separate the two, and he also rejects Hobbes's attempt to make the church subservient to the state. Irvin Ehrenpreis, *Swift: The Man, His Works, and the Age* (Cambridge: Harvard University Press, 1967), vol. 2, discusses Swift's positions on the church, the state, and their relationship. His discussion includes an analysis of *The Sentiments of a Church of England Man* (pp. 124–31).

[18]Peter Munz, *The Place of Hooker in the History of Thought* (London: Routledge and Kegan Paul, 1952), 64.

and deductive processes. According to Hooker, natural laws are "investigable by reason, without the help of Revelation supernatural and divine," but Hooker's investigation of natural laws is not advanced by Baconian empiricism or by Cartesian rationalism: "The world hath always been acquainted with them."[19] Considered after the debacle of the Puritan revolution and the increased influence of the new science, Hooker's faith in reason must have seemed old-fashioned, although a version of it survived in the Cambridge Platonists. When man is studied empirically, he may appear more or less rational, but Hooker's concept of reason is philosophically and theologically derived, not empirically discovered.

Swift's writings in defense of the relationship of church and state in England generally accord with the position of Hooker. Swift's view is that the dissolution of the connections between the sacred and the secular, church and state, spirit and body, leads to unrestrained and arbitrary individualism. Even if these connections engender constant tensions, Swift regards the abandoning of either of their terms as willful. But despite this general consonance with Hooker's view, Swift also perceives the difficulties of accepting Hooker's faith in the practical efficacy of reason in human society. Against the theoretical claims of Hooker's reason, Swift's empirical vision too makes its demands. As John Traugott observes, "Swift's radical undermining of reason and will brings into question the fundamental assumption of Hooker's church, which is that the *societas perfectus* is founded on reason and through reason, laws, both effects of God's grace."[20]

In the "Argument Against Abolishing Christianity," Swift measures the distance between Hooker's formulations and a fictional version of the condition of Christian society in England. Hooker writes: "The general and perpetual voice of men is as the sentence of God himself. For that which all men

---

[19]Richard Hooker, *Of the Laws of Ecclesiastical Polity* (London: J. M. Dent, 1907), 1: viii, 9. Subsequent references are to this edition.
[20]John Traugott, "A Tale of a Tub," in *Focus: Swift*, ed. C. J. Rawson (London: Sphere Books, 1971), 116.

have at all times learned, Nature herself must needs have taught, and God being the author of Nature, her voice is but his instrument" (1:vii, 3). Swift's speaker reduces Hooker's "general and perpetual voice" to "this Majority of Opinion": "a Design to oppose the Current of the People; which besides the Folly of it, is a manifest Breach of the Fundamental Law, that makes this Majority of Opinion the Voice of God" (2:26). The speaker of the *Argument* appears to resist the majority who wish to repeal Christianity, but his argument is an analysis of their actual practical interests, not of their mistakenly assumed ones: as Christianity has no moral effects on this majority, its few practical benefits need not be forgone. Rather than opposing the majority, he is clarifying their true interests by revealing their mistaken assumptions.

Swift's speaker directly attacks freethinkers, dissenters and, less prominently, Catholics. He himself appears to be the voice of Anglicanism, defending Christianity and, in addition, the sacramental test. But he defines a world from which Hooker's reason has vanished (although his church remains established). There is no possible appeal to a discernible natural law that connects human institutions to divine law. The speaker's defense of Christianity makes no claims that are not secular and dependent purely on human self-interest. Religion itself has become a matter not of reason that compels but of arbitrary choice: "As long as we leave in Being a God, and his Providence, with all the necessary Consequences..., we do not strike at the Root of the Evil" (2:37).

Between Hooker and Swift's speaker, an unorthodox response to the Puritan theocracy intervenes—Hobbes's *Leviathan*, "that *Mortall God*, to which wee owe under the *Immortall God*, our peace and defence."[21] The Leviathan is the sovereign who includes all, even those who oppose him: "Because the major part hath by consenting voices declared a Soveraigne; he that dissented must now consent with the rest" (II, 17, p. 231).

[21]Hobbes, *Leviathan*, ed. C. B. MacPherson (Baltimore: Penguin Books, 1968), II, 17, p. 227. All subsequent references will be to this edition, which is a reprint of the "Head" edition. Part and chapter citations are given to facilitate reference to other editions.

In a Christian commonwealth, this sovereign is God's vicere-
gent, and people should "observe for a Rule, that Doctrine,
which is the name of God, hee commanded to bee taught" (III,
36, p. 468). Hobbes's law of nature merely induces people to
arrange a peace, nothing other than self-preservation having a
claim before enforceable positive laws are created. Hobbes and
the Puritans are, in a sense, the opposites that meet. As a consequence of the radical egocentrism of their versions of humanity, religion becomes a secular power in both. Seeing people as
totally depraved, the Puritans accept a theocracy that claims
biblical authority; seeing people as totally self-interested (a secular version of total depravity), Hobbes accepts only an absolute monarch. In both cases, the end result is arbitrary power.

Hobbists, Puritans, and the physico-theologians (who aimed
to reach theological truth through the scientific study of
nature)—each attempted to find an authority that would fix the
meanings of nature and Scripture. Faced with nature, the Puritans subordinated it to Scripture, in order to provide a common standard for nature's interpretation. But then the
interpretation of Scripture too needed an authoritative basis.
The vilified Hobbes solved the problem without the appropriate sanctions of nature or Scripture. Faced with nature,
Hobbesian man invents religion as an explanation for the
causes of things—depending sometimes on "fancy," sometimes on the authority of various other people (*Leviathan*, I, 12,
p. 169). To halt this subjectivity, he then creates the commonwealth, a Leviathan to subsume him. Hobbes's solution, like
the Puritan one, merely substitutes one subjectivity for another, but it does so openly. The physico-theologians seemed to
have a solution that would escape both Hobbism and Puritan-
ism. They directly harmonized Scripture and nature, seemingly reaching a confirmation of Scripture by empirical studies
of nature. The results, as we now know, were not what the
physico-theologians intended. Instead of confirming Scripture,
they drove a wedge between it and a scientific version of nature.

To view these issues in a specifically literary context, we may
turn to John Milton, who, by Swift's time, was the salient ex-

emplar of the literary merging of the private and the sacred. Edward Said goes as far as to argue that while *The Divine Comedy* is an "implantation of the Biblical text in the here and now," *Paradise Lost* is "characterized by the intention to exceed all previous texts": "To Dante the original texts require confirmation and incarnation in what Auerbach calls the earthly world, whereas Milton sees his text aspiring to the place of inauguration, as if to protest the usurpation of the beginning place by an antecedent text."[22]

In *The Prophetic Milton,* William Kerrigan traces the tradition of the inspired poet, the *vates,* especially as the tradition undergoes the impact of the political and social upheavals of England in the seventeenth century.[23] The classical notion of the inspired poet came to be of considerable concern when Christian literature was written in the vernacular. Is poetic inspiration on Christian topics comparable to the inspiration of the prophets? Is it not heretical to regard Dante in the same context as the Psalmist? The poets of the English Renaissance were reluctant to link their inspiration directly to the divine. According to Kerrigan's analysis, Sidney, for example, regarded man as "fallen only in will" and still able to create "art with the 'erected' faculties of his intellect" (p. 56). The artist, then, does not depend on a special inspiration for the glories of his work. And Spenser's epic, Kerrigan suggests, is more appropriately regarded as claiming inspiration from Elizabeth than from God (p. 62). But after the Puritan revolution, even the linking of inspiration with patriotism was tainted: "The old vocabulary of *furor poeticus* was not different from the new vocabulary of religious revolution" (p. 72).

[22]Edward Said, *Beginnings: Intention and Method* (New York: Basic Books, 1975), 213. Said links questions of authority in literary texts with the paternal role of the author: "a begetter, beginner, father, or ancestor" (p. 83). Michael Seidel, *Satiric Inheritance: Rabelais to Sterne* (Princeton: Princeton University Press, 1979), explores the lineage of satire, finding Swift's *Tale* to be about "satirically weakened lines of descent: fathers to sons, ancients to moderns" (p. 169).

[23]William Kerrigan, *The Prophetic Milton* (Charlottesville: University Press of Virginia, 1974), especially the chapters "Prophets and Poets," "Prophets and Protestants."

34

Some opponents of the Puritans reserved inspiration exclusively for the writers of Scripture. In his "Preface" to *Gondibert*, Davenant attacked inspiration, whether poetical or political, and equated it with "enthusiasm" (in the seventeenth- and eighteenth-century sense of mental aberration). Davenant's attack on inspiration was followed by two works that treated religious inspiration, or enthusiasm, in a way that anticipated Swift's *Tale of a Tub* volume, Meric Casaubon's *A Treatise of Enthusiasme*, and Henry More's *Enthusiasmus triumphatus*.[24] Both argued the irrationality of a belief in private inspiration. But the best-known response to inspiration was that of Hobbes, whose views are reflected in Swift's depiction of the dissenters as Aeolists: "*Inspiration*. . . is nothing but the blowing into man some thin and subtile aire, or wind" (III, 17, p. 440). Even in Scripture, Hobbes asserts, the word "inspiration" is used "metaphorically only." Regarding all claims to private revelation as unverifiable, Hobbes chose to prevent anarchy by the expedient of relegating all authority to the sovereign, substituting power for inspiration.

Swift's great satires explore these issues of authority both directly and through his central fiction of the "author," with its implicit claim to the authority of inspiration, or at least insight. The contexts alter from *A Tale of a Tub* to the *Travels into Several Remote Nations of the World*, but the hermeneutical and epistemological problems remain the same. Swift shows his authors claiming the external authority of books or nature for a vision that is gradually exposed not only as private but also as solipsistic. *The self is the only thing known to exist*

[24]Clarence M. Webster, "Swift and Some Earlier Satirists of Puritan Enthusiasm," *PMLA* 48 (1933), 1141–53.

PART ONE

A Tale of a Tub

CHAPTER 2

The Hermeneutics of Self

Much of *A Tale of a Tub* deals explicitly with the interpretation of texts. The three brothers interpret their father's will, and the narrator replicates the hermeneutical themes of the tale in his digressions: critics are the subject of one of the digressions, and the putative author, who identifies himself as an expositor of modern texts, displays some of his methods of "Exantlation" (p. 67). This author defines his own writings as "miraculous," containing hidden meanings and worthy of "ample Commentaries," a scripture as commanding as the will (pp. 184, 185).[1]

---

[1] Jay Arnold Levine, "The Design of *A Tale of a Tub* (with a Digression on a Mad Modern Critic)," *ELH: A Journal of English Literary History* 33 (1966), 198–227, discusses many parallels between *A Tale of a Tub* and the issues of biblical criticism that were current in Swift's time. I differ with Levine's identification of the narrator as the debased figure of a "Bentleyan critic" (p. 200). The hermeneutical materials are used, I think, to elucidate a variety of relationships between readers and authors rather than primarily to characterize the narrator as a "modern sacred critic" (p. 206). Ronald Paulson, *Theme and Structure in Swift's "Tale of a Tub"* (New Haven: Yale University Press, 1960), identifies the central figure as a hack writer but regards "the religious theme" as "the crucial one to an understanding of the *Tale*" (p. 5). Paulson links teller to tale using the resemblance of the hack's imagination to the characteristics of Gnosticism as defined and attacked by Irenaeus, who is cited on the title page of the *Tale* (pp. 122–28). Philip Pinkus, *Swift's Vision of Evil: A Comparative Study of "A Tale of a Tub" and "Gulliver's Travels,"* English Literary Studies (Victoria, B.C.: University of Victoria, 1975), 1:57–68, surveys the history of Gnostic heresies, and, like Paulson, links the mysterious lore used by Swift's narrator to Gnosticism. Pinkus finds that "Grub

Readers are frequently enjoined to read deeply, literally, allegorically, or kindly.

The hermeneutical issues that are developed in the content are also raised by the form of the *Tale*. The text is presented as a reconstructed work of a conjectural author. There are many omitted passages inconsistently and confusingly explained, and a note remarks that "The Title Page in the Original was so torn, that it was not possible to recover several Titles which the Author here speaks of" (p. 71). Not only is the author's name omitted, but his work has multiple sources of whose authority even he remains uncertain: "Now, whether the System here delivered, was wholly compiled by *Jack,* or, as some Writers believe, rather copied from the Original at *Delphos,* with certain Additions and Emendations suited to Times and Circumstances, I shall not absolutely determine" (p. 161). Consequently the reader is presented with allegorical interpretations of the will that occur not only within another allegory but also within one of undetermined authority. Even the explanatory notes attached to this allegory sometimes announce bafflement: "I cannot guess the Author's meaning here, which I would be very glad to know, because it seems to be of Importance" (p. 191; see also p. 84).

The hermeneutical principle for rationalizing this morass (as announced in the notes and as implied in the author's "Apology," pp. 8, 12) is seemingly innocent: the meaning of the text is what the author intended. But in the very process of announcing this principle, the *Tale*'s narrator subverts it: "Whatever Reader desires to have a thorow Comprehension of an Author's Thoughts, cannot take a better Method, than by putting himself into Circumstances and Postures of Life, that the Writer was in, upon every important Passage as it flow'd from

---

Street . . . is the central metaphor of the *Tale,* joining the satires on religion and learning into one unified conception" (p. 38). Paulson, Levine, and Pinkus treat Swift's narrator as almost exclusively exemplifying what Swift mocks. While I believe that the narrator is an object of Swift's satire, I also argue that he knowingly articulates many failures of the moderns and is used to question the relationship of any author and reader.

his Pen; For this will introduce a Parity and strict Correspondence of Idea's between the Reader and the Author'' (p. 44). This announcement is the first step toward overthrowing the text, not toward interpreting it. Conceiving of a text as a way of conjoining two selves makes the meaning of the text no longer "what the author intended" but "what the author is.'' The tale-teller's emphasis causes him to dominate his text in an indeterminate way: the text represents his desires as well as his meanings. Consequently, the author's authority is exercised on the reader more than on the text. The reader must supply the meanings that correspond to the author's demands, however vague and seemingly irrelevant. If interpretation is "strict parity" between author and reader, the rigidities of a text may indeed be an impediment: "If the judicious Reader can assign a fitter [place for this digression], I do here empower him to remove it into any other Corner he pleases" (p. 149). And ultimately all demands on the text may be dissolved except for the relationship of author and reader, who are "old Acquaintance . . .loth to part": "to *write upon Nothing*" may then even be desirable (p. 208). The intermediary of a text is presumably not, after all, necessary to a relationship of selves. The absolute authority that the author attempts to exercise on the reader leads him to abandon his authority over his text. But without texts, authors are only people who wish to impose themselves on others.

The *Tale*'s narrator, aware of the evanescence of modern texts, of the power of the last writer over all previous writers, and of every book's dependence on its reader, despairs of valid interpretation, remarking tartly both on Peter's misinterpretations of the will and on the analogous failings of biblical interpreters: "But about this time it fell out, that the Learned Brother aforesaid, had read *Aristotelis Dialectica,* and especially that wonderful Piece *de Interpretatione,* which has the Faculty of teaching its Readers to find out a Meaning in every Thing but it self; like Commentators on the *Revelations,* who proceed Prophets without understanding a Syllable of the Text" (p. 85). But he converts his own skepticism into hope for his work's continued life in the interpretive skills of his readers. He invites seven scholars to work seven years at writing seven voluminous commentaries, concluding not that the commentaries will be complementary but that, whatever their differences, all will be "manifestly deduceable from the Text" (p. 185). And he claims that "*dark* Authors" are the "Lawful Parents" of meanings delivered from their texts even if they have not conceived them (p. 186).

The traditions of biblical exegesis provide the context for the narrator's claims. Questions about the nature of the authority of biblical texts are questions about the authority of the writer; is the writer's a limited human authority subsumed in a divine author, or are the texts merely authorized by their writer? The elevation of the text implicitly diminishes the writer, and the elevation of the writer implicitly diminishes the text. A similar question can be posed of secular texts: is the writer authorized by something greater than self, for example, by nature or by a prior privileged text like the Bible, or is the book only the product of a private vision, having no greater authority than its writer? Bunyan, for example, derives the authority of *The Pilgrim's Progress* from the Bible, connecting a contemporary process to a completed Scripture by means of biblical language and imagery. Furthermore, within Bunyan's book, the dream *appears* to the dreamer rather than being generated by him. The dreamer is, consequently, subordinated to the dream and the dream to Scripture. Nevertheless, authors who subordinate themselves to some greater authority claim a derived authority for themselves; their authority is that of an interpreter of a prior text, a claim both Bunyan and Milton make. Swift brings these interpretive concerns under critical scrutiny through his narrator's wisecracks and demands.

The specific interpretive issue that is most frequently raised in the *Tale* is the connection of the literal to figurative or spiritual meanings. These meanings had a long and uneasy relationship in medieval and Reformation hermeneutics, and the problems associated with discriminating between them acquired a peculiar emphasis by Swift's time as a result of the rise of empiricism and the new science. The following account is intended to define the traditional background for the manipulations of the literal and figurative by the narrator and by Peter, Jack, and Martin in the tale, and also to suggest the developments in Swift's time that kept these issues alive.[2]

Far from being the obvious, commonsensical, and uninterpreted level of the text, the literal presents the thorniest of interpretive problems. As James Preus shows, conflict arises less about the importance of the literal, which is acknowledged, than about its definition.[3] Confusion is incipient in St. Thomas Aquinas's attempts to formulate the literal, in which Preus finds three senses: "the grammatical and historical, corresponding to the intention of the human author; the divine-literal, corresponding to the intention of the divine author and unfolded piecemeal to human beings; and the traditional normative-literal, to which the spiritual senses apparently are to conform" (p. 55). (The "normative literal" is the meaning that governs or authorizes the "formation of normative religious and theological ideas," p. 4.)

These multiple meanings are only the beginning of the confusion. Aquinas located the literal sense(s) in the words and the spiritual senses in the things to which the words refer. But the referentiality of words is itself a serious problem, especially in figurative uses of language. If we make figurative language directly referential, we sometimes turn literal meaning into absurdity: "That time of year thou mayst in me behold / when yellow leaves, or few, or none do hang." Such a literal sense would be of little use in its own right. To resolve this difficulty, Aquinas makes the literal conform to the author's intention. But if God intends both the words and the things, then is the

---

[2]The subsequent pages deal with facets of biblical interpretation that were, at least in general, widely known in Swift's time. Among relevant books listed in the sale catalog of Swift's library are Aquinas's *Summa theologiae,* Calvin's *Institutes of the Christian Religion,* Hooker's *Of the Laws of Ecclesiastical Polity,* and Simon's *Histoire critique de vieux Testament.* See Harold Williams, *Dean Swift's Library* (London: Cambridge University Press, 1932). And as Phillip Harth, *Swift and Anglican Rationalism: The Religious Background of "A Tale of a Tub"* (Chicago: University of Chicago Press, 1961), has shown, Swift was well versed in Anglican apologetics.

[3]James Preus, *From Shadow to Promise: Old Testament Interpretation from Augustine to the Young Luther* (Cambridge: Harvard University Press, 1969).

spiritual sense too not literal? Otherwise the interpreter must rely on the merely human writer in his history-bound context for a definition of the literal.

Such complexities suggest the uneasiness of the relationship between the historical and the literal. Either the literal is reduced to the historical and is regarded as relatively insignificant except as it figures spiritual meanings, or the literal becomes itself the bearer of a meaning that has little connection to the historical. The Reformation was unique not in focusing attention on the literal, which had already received enormous attention, but in its insistence on uniting the historical and the spiritual within the literal.

In Luther's late commentaries on the Psalms, he attends to the specific historical situation of the speaker, a focus that would have deprived the Psalms of theological interest for many previous readers. Luther regards the Old Testament faithful as looking forward to the coming of Christ, however, just as Christians look forward to their own final redemption. In this view, the spiritual promises of the Old Testament can be included in the literal level and can also exist within their own historical context. In Preus's words, "The Old Testament gets theological value not so much from the Christ it hiddenly describes as from the salvation it promises" (p. 186).

Swift's generation was caught between a biblical interpretation that it regarded as obscurantist and one that reduced Scripture to secular history.[4] Hans Frei identifies the writing of

'Roland E. Bainton, "The Bible in the Reformation," in *The Cambridge History of the Bible*, ed. S. L. Greenslade (London: Cambridge University Press, 1963), 3:1–37, provides a useful survey of major issues in biblical interpretation. Victor Harris, "Allegory to Analogy in the Interpretation of Scriptures," *Philological Quarterly* 45 (1966), 1–23, studies the reduced confidence in the allegorical tradition and the "introduction of empirical criteria in order to test literal meaning or historical truth" (p. 8), stating that typology became "a form of literal truth and a substitute for allegory" (p. 10). Paul J. Korshin, "The Development of Abstracted Typology in England, 1650–1820," in *Literary Uses of Typology from the Late Middle Ages to the Present*, ed. Earl Miner (Princeton: Princeton University Press, 1979), 147–203, surveys uses of typology in other than specifically theological contexts. Korshin emphasizes the blurring of theological and hermeneutical distinctions in the eighteenth century: "Types, emblems, symbols, hieroglyphics—all come to be used synonymously" (p. 154).

Anthony Collins, Swift's contemporary and the object of his scorn, as a striking illustration of a new interpretive situation.[5] Collins "assigned the origin of specific meaning to the intention of the individual author," and he identified the meaning of a statement with the "state of affairs to which it refers" because the meanings of words are derived from sense experience (Frei, p. 78). Although Collins's writings were too late to affect *A Tale of a Tub,* they extend a conception of meaning and interpretation that was growing throughout the seventeenth century. Frei describes this conception as follows: "Why scan the heavens speculatively when from the written word, from the knowledge of historical conditions and the way human beings think, one can ascertain with great probability what the immediate and human rather than the remote divine author had in mind?" pp. 78–79). The view that Collins represents contrasts sharply with the biblical exegesis exemplified and codified in Augustine and Aquinas. Collins's specific attack, however, is on the Reformed interpretation of his own time. And in a sense his views are an extension of the emphasis on the literal meaning that is the salient characteristic of Reformed interpretation as it developed from Luther and Calvin.

The Reformer's emphasis on the literal tends to limit meaning to the intention of the writer and, consequently, leads eventually to the assumption of Collins that anything undiscoverable by the historical-critical method is not there. Collins scornfully rejects assertions that the Old Testament contains prophecies of Christ: "Advocates for the Christian religion,

[5]Hans Frei, *The Eclipse of Biblical Narrative: A Study of Eighteenth- and Nineteenth-Century Hermeneutics* (New Haven: Yale University Press, 1974), 66. Readers of Swift are likely to know Collins's *A Discourse of Free-Thinking* (1713), a work parodied by Swift in *Mr. Collins's Discourse of Free-Thinking Put into Plain English By Way of Abstract, for the Use of the Poor* (1713). Collins addresses many issues of biblical interpretation in his discourse, including text, canon, readings, and translation (pp. 50–99). He is contemptuous of the interpretive ingenuities of the defenders of orthodox Christianity who argue "that there are many places of Scripture which have a double Sense, a Literal and a Spiritual. And both these Senses are subdivided: For the Literal Sense is natural or figurative; and the Spiritual is sometimes allegorical, sometimes anagogical; nay, sometimes there are divers literal Senses in the same Sentence" (pp. 58–59).

45

both ancient and modern, have judged them to be applied in a secondary, or typical, or mystical, or allegorical, or enigmatical sense; that is, in a sense different from the obvious and literal sense, which they bear in the Old Testament."⁶ Collins's point of view denies, or at least limits the concept of providential history that supports typology. For Augustine a historical narrative is not to be considered a human institution, "because those things which are past and cannot be revoked belong to the order of time, whose creator and administrator is God."⁷ And Aquinas remarks that God has the power, not only of adapting "words to convey meanings (which men can also do), but also of adapting things themselves."⁸ Consequently, for them biblical history may be both prefigurative and descriptive of a contemporaneous event, while for Collins it is bound to its time.

Even before Collins, both Hobbes and some of Hobbes's opponents had carried the Reformed tendency toward literal interpretation to an astonishing extreme. Hobbes's biblical interpretation, which is extensive, is as materialistic as his philosophy. His transformations of the terms of spirit to physical entities verge on the parodic. But the physico-theologians, Hobbes's enemies, developed their own forms of literal interpretation, making Scripture accord with science. Scriptural interpretation came to depend on a knowledge of second causes, with a diminished reliance on a providential scheme in which the temporal finds its place in the eternal. These new readings of nature and Scripture aim to be as univocal as a Royal Society tract. Thomas Burnet, a physico-theologian attacked by Swift, argued in *The Sacred Theory of the Earth* that Scripture can only be understood in the terms now unveiled by the new science. In his view, the creation, the flood, and the final conflagration had remained mysterious until the operations of nature were comprehended by the science of his time. Augustine and

⁶Anthony Collins, *A Discourse of the Grounds and Reasons of the Christian Religion* (London, 1737), 35. Quoted in Frei, *The Eclipse of Biblical Narrative,* 68–69.

⁷St. Augustine, *On Christian Doctrine,* trans. D. W. Roberts, Jr. (New York: Liberal Arts Press, 1958), 64. All subsequent references are to this edition.

⁸St. Thomas Aquinas, *Summa theologiae,* ed. Thomas Gilby, O.P. (New York: McGraw-Hill, 1965), 1:38–39. All subsequent references are to this edition.

Aquinas too had moved from signs to things, but the "things" enlarged God's book. Their literal was an authorial meaning, not a physically apprehendable material, and this meaning expanded as the reader moved from sign to thing.

In a secularized world, the referent of language tends to be identified as the literal. Through this referential literal, language is linked to a nature that is regarded as if it opposed spirit. But when language is separated from referent, the literal becomes lettoral, language too having its own body as well as spirit.[9] In a secularized world, book, words, letters, and metaphors too assert themselves against spirit. Swift explores literalization in both these ways, that is, as a reduction of a word to its secularly defined physical referent and also to its letter.

The narrator of the *Tale* and the brothers in his tale use literalization and figuration as interpretive strategies to bend texts to their purposes. Wishing to satirize critics, the narrator appropriates the statement "their Writings are the Mirrors of Learning" (p. 102). He remarks quite sensibly: "This I understand in a literal Sense, and suppose our Author must mean, that whoever designs to be a perfect Writer, must inspect into the Books of *Criticks,* and correct his Invention there as in a Mirror" (pp. 102–103). With impeccable method he first interprets the literal as the author's meaning and then interprets the things to which the author refers: he remarks that "the *Mirrors* of the Antients were made of *Brass,* and *sine Mercurio*" (p. 103). He has skillfully derived this satirical remark about critics from a statement whose literal meaning appears to be opposed to his allegorical—or spiritual, in Aquinas's sense—interpretation. The narrator later refers to those "whose peculiar Talent lies in fixing Tropes and Allegories to the *Letter,* and refining what is Literal into Figure and Mystery" (p. 190), a confounding of literal and figurative that is evident early in the three brothers' careers. Peter decides that "the same Word which in the Will is

---

[9]Maureen Quilligan, *The Language of Allegory: Defining the Genre* (Ithaca: Cornell University Press, 1979), defines the literal as follows: "The truly literal meaning of 'literal' is, in fact, not 'actual,' 'real,' or 'lifelike,' but 'lettoral'—having to do with the reading of letters grouped into words as in the sense of 'literate' " (p. 67).

called *Fringe,* does also signifie a *Broomstick"* (p. 88). One of the brothers objects that the attached epithet "silver" applies to fringe but not to broomstick. Peter responds that "silver" must be "understood in a *Mythological,* and *Allegorical* Sense" (p. 88).

Literalization, in its ultimate "lettoral" sense, is returning the book to its status as a physical object, and allegorization ultimately implies replacing the book with a meaning. These processes manifest themselves in a rudimentary form when the brothers reduce the Will to letters, then recombine the letters into a new meaning (pp. 83–84). The brothers literalize to free themselves of the text and then allegorize to make a subsequent meaning fit their purpose. And they dissolve the text not only by literalizing and allegorizing it but also by historicizing it: "These Figures were not all the *same* with those that were formerly worn, and were meant in the Will. Besides they did not wear them in that Sense, as forbidden by their Father" (p. 89). This first phase of the Will's misinterpretation ends with its being locked up. Although its author's will is then prevented from interfering with his sons' wills, the Will does retain a physical integrity. Its final perversion occurs when Jack makes it only a material to serve his own will: "He had a Way of working it into any Shape he pleased; so that it served him for a night-cap when he went to Bed, and for an Umbrello in rainy Weather. He would lap a Piece of it around a sore Toe, or when he had Fits, burn two Inches under his Nose" (p. 190).

The relationship of readers to this seemingly sophistical hermeneutical exercise is double: they perceive the brothers' failures but themselves engage in interpreting a text that so complicates the hermeneutical issues as to make the brothers' efforts seem almost simpleminded. The narrator announces that the Will "consisted wholly in certain plain, easy Directions about the management and wearing of their Coats"; however, Jack makes the matter "*deeper* and *darker*" (p. 190). This principle of simplicity appears to be a way of marking the brothers' perversions: all difficulties are the result of willful obfuscations of the obvious. But the reader's experience has not been one of obviousness. The story of the three brothers is allegory and does not mean what it says; even the notes sometimes admit bafflement. And when this allegory is itself allegorized or literalized by the brothers, the reader's need to balance the double equations of the allegory verges on the maddening. The transformation of fringe into broomstick is ludicrous because one literal is turned into another irrelevant literal. But although fringe is literal to them in their story, to us it is allegorical (Swift's footnote: "This is certainly the farther introducing the Pomps of Habit and Ornament" [p. 88]). Surely a silver broomstick is as adequate a vehicle as silver fringe to denote pomp. The reason for prohibiting the reading of "broomsticks" is that literal broomsticks cannot be worn on literal coats. The coats, however, are no more literal than the fringe.

The tortured allegorical interpretation recommended in the *Tale* is often defined by the narrator as typological, a version of the figural. In the biblical figural, a historical event of the Old Testament is regarded as prefiguring another historical event of the New Testament, as well as an event or condition still to be fulfilled. The literary use of the figural depends on the presumption that there is a coincidence of the order of the text with that of nature or history outside the text. The typological or figural is a pattern of repetition that is fertile, that multiplies meaning rather than reiterates it. But the *Tale* opens out not on nature or history but only on other books that are allotted no more authority than it has. The narrator is persuaded of the exhaustion of nature and abandons himself to the assistance of his commonplace book. In the "Digression on Madness," he explicitly divorces the world of nature from that of fiction. Typology then becomes mere repetition. Although the *Tale* contains the claim that it is a completion of others' books—Homer's, for example (p. 127)—neglecting nothing "that can be of Use upon any Emergency of Life" (p. 129), it is more inclusively conceived as a book that exemplifies the modern author's method of making a book by "transcribing from others and disgressing from himself" (p. 148). The implication is clear that learning is being dissipated rather than accumulated: "Tho' Authors need be little consulted, yet *Criticks,* and *Commentators,* and *Lexicons* carefully must" (p. 148).

The *Tale* gradually creates a sense that its hermeneutical lore is there not only to be mocked but also to provide a means of self-definition for its narrator-"author." He reads us, himself, the world, into it and through it. The patristic schemes for finding one's place in a universe and one's time in eternity are transformed into devices for self-enclosure. This activity has its analogy within Christianity. Protestant Christians often extended the type from past history to include themselves as part of a typological pattern founded in Scripture.[10] But when a figural system is used to reorder the evanescent events of a private life, the interpreter, not the implicit historical relationships, becomes the device for uniting these disparate events. The very notion of defining oneself in terms of biblical typology implies a subjective understanding of the relationship. The interpreter becomes creator.

The tale-teller's literalizing and allegorizing is a device for locating himself in the narrow space between freedom and formlessness. His interpretations suggest the arbitrary, the private, but they also confine him to a book. The hiatuses, prefaces and notes of the *Tale* emphasize its literal as letter, as body, as fixed, while the tale-teller allegorizes, spiritualizes, frees its meanings. Rather than attempting to reconcile letter and spirit, the narrator of the *Tale* emphasizes the extremes of the physical and spiritual oppositions contained in the notion of a book: a modern book is "a very comely Figure on a Bookseller's Shelf, there to be preserved neat and clean, for a long Eternity, adorn'd with the Heraldry of its Title, fairly inscribed on a Label; never to be thumb'd or greas'd by Students, nor bound to Everlasting Chains of Darkness in a Library: But when the Fulness of time is come, shall haply undergo the Tryal of Purgatory in order *to ascend the Sky*" (p. 148). His biting re-

---

[10]The figural and its relationship to history are developed in Erich Auerbach, "Figura," in *Scenes from the Drama of European Literature,* trans. Ralph Manheim (New York: Meridian Books, 1959). Barbara Lewalski, *Protestant Poetics and the Seventeenth-Century Religious Lyric* (Princeton: Princeton University Press, 1979), comments that Protestants were invited to see salvation history "recapitulated in their lives" (p. 131). J. Paul Hunter, *The Reluctant Pilgrim: Defoe's Emblematic Method and Quest for Form in "Robinson Crusoe"* (Baltimore: Johns Hopkins University Press, 1966), chap. 6, discusses the various literary forms by which Puritans connected their lives to biblical patterns.

marks about a modern book are also an exemplification of his own interpretive procedures, which are designed to house his uneasy spirit in a body of paper.

The equation of a book to a person or a world is a familiar one. The Word is incarnate, and God's works are a book of nature; both are interpreted through the written word. When a secular book and a world are equated, the author is analogous to God. Through imagination or verisimilitude the author may be able to create a world that surpasses or rivals this one; he may, however, be able only to purvey some degraded version of this world. Thus, when human limitation rather than divinely instilled power becomes the focus of attention, the reader is reminded that the human analogue to God the Creator is a mere person who writes a book.

The book of God's works includes the book of his creatures, one of which is man. As microcosm, the creature may imply much more than himself. Nevertheless, the analogy of person and book, apparently so much less grand than that of world and book, is also susceptible to a deflating interpretation. This analogy may imply a shrinking and distorting process rather than the revelation of the large in the small. The book that is a person may then be a reification of the limits and perversions of self. From a secular perspective, writers' representations of themselves in their books may appear to be their only valid activity. But in a world that acknowledges an obligation to transhuman values, this arrogation of a book by self may also appear to be an unseemly pretense to divinity.

The eighteenth century became increasingly hospitable to the analogy of a book to a person.[11] Writing as a preservation or creation of self is a common conception, Sterne's *Tristram Shandy* and Boswell's *London Journal* being perhaps the salient examples. *A Tale of a Tub, Tristram Shandy,* and *London Journal* encapsulate an otherwise unstable self in the fixities of a book. What is preserved is change and indefinition. In some ways these books oppose narrative, subverting its continuous motion

[11]Patricia Meyer Spacks, *Imagining a Self: Autobiography and Novel in Eighteenth-Century England* (Cambridge: Harvard University Press, 1976), discusses the burgeoning of literary creations of identity in the period.

by their withdrawal into an inner world. But this inner world has itself the motion and dispersal of narrative. Instead of positing a stable human agent in a giddy world, these books transfer the instability of the world to the agent. Still, the tolerant attitude toward the literary creation of the self that is exemplified in Sterne and Boswell more nearly resembles that of Montaigne than that of Swift, who attacks the attempt to evade human limitations by creating a fictional identity.

The putative author of *A Tale of a Tub* attempts to reduce the world to his own limits. He aims to achieve a close connection, even a physical identity, of self, world, and book: "I shall here pause awhile, till I find, by feeling the World's Pulse, and my own, that it will be of absolute Necessity for us both, to resume my Pen" (p. 210). He even presents himself as a version of the Word: "Since my *Vein* is once opened, I am content to exhaust it all at a Running, for the Peculiar Advantage of my dear Country, and for the universal Benefit of Mankind" (p. 184). Gulliver, in contrast, conceives of his book as the world; the *Travels,* he claims, is objective and definitive, in contrast to people, who are partial and tentative. Gulliver attempts to extend the limits of his humanity by subjecting himself to a discipline of objectivity that reflects the doctrines espoused by the Royal Society. But finally he too is a man who has written only a book, not a scripture. Both Gulliver and the tale-teller attempt to evade the limits of humanity, the tale-teller aggrandizing self instead of trying to subjugate it to some conception of the objective.

Before Swift's time, the most prominent secular example of a book representing a person was Montaigne's *Essays*: "Myself am the matter of my book"; "my kinsfolk and friends...may therein recover some traits of my conditions and humours, and by that means preserve more whole, and more life-like, the

[12]*The Essays of Michel Eyquem de Montaigne,* trans. Charles Cotton, ed. W. Carew Hazlitt (Chicago: Encyclopaedia Britannica, 1952). Volume and essay numbers are given in the text. Cotton's translation first appeared in 1685–86. Kathleen Williams, *Jonathan Swift and the Age of Compromise* (Lawrence: University of Kansas Press, 1958), notes a number of parallels between Swift's thought and Montaigne's, especially in relation to their conceptions of reason. Ronald Paulson, *Theme and Structure in Swift's "Tale of a Tub"* (New Ha-

knowledge they had of me" ("The Author to the Reader").[12]
But as Richard Regosin argues, this equation of book and self
is not modest: "The role [Montaigne] takes on and the action
he sets out ring out with distant echoes of divinity. . . . as God is
to be found in His book, so Montaigne resides in his."[13]

The *Essays* made available to Swift an intense exploration of
the relationships of the observing subject to the external world
and of the potentialities and liabilities of self. While it appears
certain that Swift was strongly influenced by Montaigne, I am
not, in my discussion here, asserting that every cited passage is
a source for some idea of Swift's. The *Essays* are a precursor to
the *Tale,* and an understanding of them is as much an aid to our
reading of the *Tale* as it was to Swift's writing of it.

The susceptibility of self to literary re-creation is a recurrent
theme of the book. Each of Montaigne's essays has a subject
matter other than self, but all seemingly external content becomes part of his representation of self. Montaigne finds an obvious characteristic of the self to be its disorder, its resistance to
being subdued to definition. But Montaigne submerges himself
in his subjectivity rather than attempting to evade or deny it:
"I turn my sight inwards, and there fix and employ it. I have
no other business but myself, I am eternally meditating upon
myself" (Montaigne, II, 17, p. 320). He finds the external orders imposed by literature and philosophy to be fallacious. Authors mistakenly "choose a general air of man, and according
to that interpret all his actions," and "even the best authors

---

ven: Yale University Press, 1960), sees Montaigne as central to the tradition
that made Swift's *Tale* possible: "Montaigne intends, by showing that man's
only basis for certainty is his own subjective opinion, to prove man's inadequacy and need for the authority of common forms; but this emphasis is very
easily shifted to an exaltation of the individual's subjective opinion. An un-
derlying assumption in seventeenth-century literature that must not be dis-
counted is the ever-growing interest in self, derived in part from Renaissance
humanism and in part from the trend toward subjectivity manifested in all
branches of the Protestant Reformation" (p. 8). My concern here is with the
rather narrow area of self and book in Montaigne, which I think made possible Swift's articulation of a number of important themes in the *Tale.*

[13]Richard Regosin, *The Matter of My Book: Montaigne's "Essais" as the Book of
the Self* (Berkeley: University of California Press, 1977), 151.

[are] a little out in so obstinately endeavouring to make of us any constant and solid contexture" (Montaigne, II, 1, p. 159). Thus Montaigne uses his volume to create an order, not of consistency, but of unsuppressed inconsistency brought into the compass of a vast book. The *Essays* provide a prototype for some aspects of the *Tale*'s form and an exposition of some of its principal themes.

The issue that Montaigne raises so forcefully concerns personal identity. What sense of connection is there among all of these contradictions: "I do not only find it hard to piece our actions to one another, but I, moreover, find it hard properly to design each by itself by any principal quality, so ambiguous and variform they are, with diverse lights" (Montaigne, III, 13, p. 522). He quotes Lucretius, who, like Locke, attributes our sense of continuity to memory (Montaigne, II, 12, p. 249), but Montaigne claims that he himself has a defective memory (Montaigne, I, 9, p. 15).

Montaigne's *Essays* create the personal identity that he cannot define logically or assume through memory. Whatever his contradictions, his "book is always the same" (Montaigne, III, 9, p. 466). The book defines him by accretion. It encompasses his inconsistencies, not resolving them into the fictional consistency of a moment, but providing a record of the incongruencies of the self through time. Looking over the interpolations in his *Essays*, Montaigne remarks: "I now, and I anon, are two several persons; but whether better, I cannot determine" (Montaigne, III, 9, p. 466). He perceives in himself not a movement toward improvement but rather a "drunken, stumbling, reeling, infirm motion" (Montaigne, III, 9, p. 466).

Montaigne in his library on the third floor of a tower is a dignified version of Swift's hack in a garret. He spends his time leafing through books "without method or design," at intervals setting down "such whimsies as these I present to you here" (Montaigne, III, 3, p. 400). Montaigne's withdrawal into self, and the fragmentariness of his reading and writing correspond to his perception of his life and his book. His writing transforms the fragments of his reading, not into an extended order, but into nodules of meaning that represent a constantly changing conception of an evanescent self.

The relationship between book and self is reciprocal. Montaigne does not simply shape a book to stand for himself; the book also shapes Montaigne:

> In moulding this figure upon myself, I have been so often constrained to temper and compose myself in a right posture, that the copy is truly taken, and has in some sort formed itself; painting myself for others, I represent myself in a better colouring than my own natural complexion. I have no more made my book, than my book has made me: 'tis a book consubstantial with the author, of a peculiar design, a member of my life, and whose business is not designed for others, as that of all other books is. [Montaigne, II, 18, p. 323]

To achieve this "consubstantiality," Montaigne rejects the conventional order of writing, making his book instead a "faggoting up of so many divers pieces" (Montaigne, II, 37, p. 365).[14] He does not form it into beginning, middle, and end but will keep on "so long as there shall be ink and paper" (Montaigne, III, 9, p. 457).

The *Essays'* independence of any ordering principle other than Montaigne's mind is achieved progressively. At first, Montaigne had seen the essays as a possibility for controlling his mind: the mind must be kept "applied to some certain study," or it will thrash about "in the vague expanse of the imagination" (Montaigne, I, 9, p. 14). But despite his writing, he recognizes that his mind continues to create "chimeras and fantastic monsters" (Montaigne, I, 9, p. 15). Later, however, he has neither hope nor desire that his writings will order or control his mind. No matter what external matter he studies, " 'tis to apply it to or rather in myself" (Montaigne, II, 6, p. 180). And rather than being ashamed of his mind, he riotously indulges its eccentricity in his later essays. "On Some Verses of

[14]Regosin, *The Matter of My Book,* explores the theological implications of Montaigne's use of "consubstantial" and of related terms (pp. 151-52).

Virgil," for example, moves by verbal association, not by analysis of an announced subject matter.

To create his tale-teller, Swift adapted the analysis of subjectivity to be found in Montaigne's book to the display of a different version of self. The self displayed in Montaigne's book is inexplicably generous as well as selfish, kind as well as cruel. The self displayed in the *Tale* is a raw and inexorable demand for gratification that seems to have specificity only because it grapples for whatever is available. Montaigne makes the point that his demonstrated and fascinating egocentricity disqualifies him (and others) from changing the social and religious customs of society. His subjectivity is not a strategy for reordering the external world but a release from having to do so. In contrast, the tale-teller aims to dominate his world: he writes his book to establish his superiority, not to investigate himself. His book's complexity results from his greed for praise, not from long self-analysis. The self that appears is impoverished; nevertheless, it is lodged in a book, as Montaigne had shown it might be.[15]

Like Montaigne, the tale-teller can "transplant" his many borrowings and can "confound" them with his own writings (Montaigne, II, 10, p. 194). He uses the mock encomium and the story of the three brothers to establish an ordered narrative pattern, but his pattern, like the subjects of Montaigne's essays, is gradually absorbed by the centripetal force of the narrator's mind. Self-expression dissolves the very conventions of writing. Any momentary order can be resolved into another by

[15]John O. Lyons, *The Invention of the Self: The Hinge of Consciousness in the Eighteenth Century* (Carbondale: Southern Illinois University Press, 1978), studies the change in the conception of the self in the later eighteenth century. His investigation is not, however, of the invention of the self but of the attachment of value to a certain version of the self: e.g., "For good or ill Rousseau was the harbinger of ideas that have formed the modern consciousness. And the most important of these ideas is that a person is not to be defined in terms of how he has conformed a primitive self to the demands of his world, but how he has imaginatively restructured his world to conform to him" (p. 104). It appears to me that many of the writers that Lyons assumes have no interest in the self (such as Swift and Defoe) have an intense interest in the self; that a writer believes the notion of an *autonomous* self to be delusion in no way inhibits his conceptualization of a self.

a word, a chance association. Memory erects no obstacles. The self can be shaped for any purpose, but the only identity is that given by the book's accretion of a multitude of selves. Montaigne's excremental image for his essays is one that Swift too later used as an oblique description of egocentricity: "And yet I have seen a gentleman who only communicated his life by the workings of his belly: you might see in his house a show of a row of basins of seven or eight day's excrements; that was all his study, all his discourse; all other talk stunk in his nostriles. Here, but not so nauseous, are the excrements of an old mind, sometimes thick, sometimes thin, and always indigested" (Montaigne, III, 9, p. 457).

When a secular book such as Montaigne's is conceived in relation to the metaphor of a person, its unity is analogous to personal identity; content and form are comprehended by techniques related to those that we use to identify people. And the organizational patterns that we impose on such a book depend to some degree on our version of the identity of the real or putative author. The tale-teller's identity is Hobbesian. Although Montaigne provides the formal basis for Swift's analysis of his putative author, the self displayed in the *Tale* is similar to that implied by the *Leviathan*.

Swift shows not that Hobbes's psychological analysis is invalid but that it is valid too often. Hobbes's political theory is derived from his assumption that people have the same passions—"*desire, feare, hope,* etc.*"*; they are differentiated from each other only by the "*objects* of the passions."[16] Unlike Montaigne's self, the self that Hobbes perceives by introspection is a collection not so much of qualities as of energies. Hobbes rejects the Epicurean notion that happiness can be achieved through tranquillity of mind: "For there is no such thing as perpetuall Tranquillity of mind, while we live here; because Life it selfe is but Motion, and can never be without Desire, nor without Feare, no more than without Sense" (*Leviathan*, I, 6, p. 130). Although the Tale's narrator desires the "Serene

[16]Hobbes, *Leviathan*, ed. C. B. MacPherson (Baltimore: Penguin Books, 1968), 83 (introduction).

Peaceful State" of Epicureanism in the "Digression on Madness," he is aware that such a state is illusory. He exhibits what Hobbes calls "a generall inclination of all mankind, a perpetuall and restless desire of Power after power, that ceaseth only in Death" (*Leviathan*, I, ii, p. 161). In his final condition, he resembles the spitefulness and fragmentation characteristic of Hobbesian man when he is not dominated by some external authority.

The precarious personal unity that Hobbes defines in his psychology is replicated in his politics. Indeed, Hobbes's politics is presented as a set of analogies between a natural and an artificial person.[17] An artificial person is any group that yields its right to act individually and acts as one: for example, the family may unite under the father if it is not part of some greater commonwealth (*Leviathan*, II, 20, p. 257). If a great state unites as one, it is a Leviathan, the giant of Hobbes's title page, who is composed of natural persons. Hobbes uses the analogies between natural and artificial persons as the means by which a monarchy is understood and justified.

The unity that Hobbes expounds is not simply that of a common purpose or customs: it is a unity as literal as that which a natural person has. The attempt to accommodate a private unity to the unity of a commonwealth creates conflict, however: "A naturall man receiveth his experience, from the naturall objects of sense, which work upon him without passion, or interest of their own; whereas they that give Counsell to the Representative person of a Common-wealth, may have, and have often their particular ends, and passions, that render their

[17]John Seelye, "Hobbes' *Leviathan* and the Giantism Complex in the First Book of *Gulliver's Travels*," *Journal of English and Germanic Philology* 60 (1961), 228–39, analyzes the conceit of giantism in the *Travels* and compares the title page of the *Leviathan* to scenes in the *Travels*. Alan S. Fisher, "An End to the Renaissance: Erasmus, Hobbes, and *A Tale of a Tub*," *Huntington Library Quarterly* 38 (1974), argues that the "Digression on Madness" defines the human condition according to the Hobbist paradigm: "If indeed we believe in Hobbes' world (and accept it), then folly and knavery are the only choices" (p. 19).

Counsells alwayes suspected, and many times unfaithfull" (*Leviathan*, II, 25, pp. 306–307). This conflict is obviated in the sovereign himself, in whom natural and artificial persons are coincident. The sovereign as both individual and Leviathan makes an identity of Hobbes's analogies.

The literalness of Hobbes's use of this analogy raises the possibility of reasoning not just from his natural to his artificial person but also from his artificial to his natural person. Perhaps a person is no more tightly organized than is Leviathan. Furthermore, this analogy of natural and artificial calls attention to the erosion of the distinction between the conventionally organic and the mechanical in Hobbes's system: "For what is the *Heart*, but a *Spring;* and the *Nerves,* but so many *Strings;* and the *Joynts*, but so many *Wheeles*, giving motion to the whole Body, such as was intended by the Artificer" (Intro., p. 81).

This confusion of the natural and artificial is apparent in the analysis of the brain in Swift's *Mechanical Operation of the Spirit.* Swift's Hobbist narrator dissolves the brain into parts as one would a mechanism, but he then animates the parts. The brain is a collection of creatures "like the Picture of *Hobbes's Leviathan*, or like the Bees in perpendicular swarm upon a Tree, or like a Carrion corrupted into Vermin, still preserving the Shape and Figure of the Mother Animal" (*Tale*, p. 277). These creatures produce various kinds of mental activity, depending on how they bite other parts of you. In a diseased condition analogous to the often-described diseases of Leviathan, will these parts of Hobbes's natural but nevertheless mechanical person perhaps enact their own roles governed only by their individual demands?

When Swift's tale-teller loses confidence in the goals that provided the foci for his diversity, he disintegrates into his components. He is delivered over to his momentary motions, and his impulses toward power become increasingly ineffectual. Deprived of his organizing assumptions, or more properly of his drives, the tale-teller has no center for personal reorganization and subordination. Having neglected the warnings issued by his sense of "his private Infirmities" and having suppressed his knowledge of the "stubborn Ignorance of the People" (*Tale*, p. 171), he is now abandoned to himself.

To summarize, in the *Tale*, Swift exposes the poverty of self by using Montaigne's method of examination: the external world is gradually subordinated to the perceiving subject. Yet the self that is revealed proves to be not Montaigne's in its ineluctable complexity but that defined by Hobbes. The increasing failure of form in the *Tale* mimes not the variousness of self but its chaos. It becomes energy without form, entropic. Ironically, the narrator's attempt to create an identity through his book succeeds as his book fragments. The *Tale*'s emphasis on the physical characteristics of printed books—their incompletely assimilated prefaces and footnotes, their interchangeable chapters—implies a body inadequately informed by a spirit.[18] The narrator attempts to transform traditional biblical interpretation into a private hermeneutical system, which will meet his demands for both freedom and identity. His demands for hermeneutical freedom, however, result in a book whose failures of form represent the disintegration of a coherent self.

[18]Ernst Curtius, *European Literature and the Latin Middle Ages,* trans. Willard R. Trask (New York: Harper and Row, 1953), 302–47, discusses the background that is relevant to this discussion in a chapter entitled "The Book as Symbol." Beryl Smalley, *The Study of the Bible in the Middle Ages,* 2d ed. (Oxford: Basil Blackwell, 1952), 2, states that in biblical exegesis the scholar "understood the relationship between letter and spirit in the same way as he did the relationship between body and soul." Hugh Kenner, *Flaubert, Joyce, Beckett: The Stoic Comedians* (Boston: Beacon Press, 1962), finds that *"A Tale of a Tub* is the first comic exploitation of that technological space which the words in a large printed book inhabit" (p. 39).

CHAPTER 3

Subduing a Literary Form

In the *Tale* Swift attacks the house of fiction with its "Artificial *Mediums,* false Lights, refracted angles, Varnish, and Tinsel," a refusal to look into the "Glass of Nature" (p. 172). He exposes the illusions that are harbored even within the ironies of satire. The *Tale* mimes an author's attempt to create a structure independent of nature, to attach the authority that the poem borrows from God to a small construction that opens inward on emptiness rather than to one that opens outward on a universe.

In early portions of the *Tale,* the narrator is an ironic commentator who appears to share the values of the kind of author implied by the text. But when in "The Digression on Madness" he denies the premises that made his satiric commentary possible, he is sharply separated from the implied author. The narrator renounces his role as discriminator, and that role is assumed by an implied, but silent, author whose services were not as urgently needed when the narrator appeared to be enacting a more comprehensive authorial role.

"The Digression on Madness" leaves before us, then, a question about the interpretation of the narrator: Do we revise our estimate of him and his tale to make all parts of the text self-consistent? If we perceive him as a mimesis of a certain kind of consciousness late in the text, do we then read that perception into an earlier part of the text? Any solution is suspect if Swift's most general attack is on our propensity for making self-indulgent fictions. Turning the satiric text into a mere example of its narrator's condition is to remove our posteriors from the range of its whip, and delivering ourselves to its narrator's vision is to acquiesce in his definition of felicity, "being a Fool among Knaves" (p. 174). Our interpretive procedures are themselves brought within the *Tale*'s purview.[1]

A reader's desire for consistency in a narrator is related to the need to posit a stable authorial position from which to interpret a text's meanings. Especially in a work of presumed polemical import, we wish to be able to define the narrator, at least crudely, as rhetorical or mimetic, as primarily a plausible exponent of the work's polemical concerns or as an exemplification of them. Either kind of narrator implies an author whose control of the text is unquestioned. But when the narrator, from his position as a facilitator of ironies directed externally, moves to a new position as an object of the irony, a question arises about the stability of the authorial position.

Although the search for the real author may be quixotic ("Don't puzzle me," responds author Tristram Shandy to interrogation), it is this quest that rhetorical schemes rationalize and order. The search for the author and his context is encouraged even more by satire than by most other kinds of fiction, and it is especially encouraged by Swift's *Tale*. Because satire assumes the prerogative of commenting on existents external and prior to itself, the interpretive strategy that it suggests is to define a historical author writing to a historical reader about historical events. In sharing, or pretending to share, a border with polemic, satire urges its reader toward a truth that applies

[1]Henry W. Sams, "Swift's Satire of the Second Person," *ELH: A Journal of English Literary History* 26 (1959), 36–44, argues that Swift induces the reader "to adopt a position which he will later be forced to abandon" (p. 41). The reader is not merely led to a new position but "compelled to be aware of the revision" (p. 41). Stanley Fish, "Literature in the Reader: Affective Stylistics," *New Literary History* 2 (1971–72), 123–62, has cogently argued the importance of "an analysis of the developing responses of the reader in relation to the words as they succeed one another in time" (pp. 126–27). The developing responses that Swift's writings induce lead the reader, I think, to be self-conscious about his or her responses, concerned with their relationships to previous responses as well as with their immediacy.

outside the borders of its text. The prominent hermeneutical concerns within the *Tale* imply that our goal should be the author's meaning, not the meaning of some diminished version of the author. The brothers are obligated to a concern with what the real author meant, not with what kind of author is implied by the Will. Furthermore, the narrator's frequent discussions of the author-reader relationship keep the hermeneutical concern of meaning as authorial intention prominent in the reader's mind. The narrator's subordination of meaning to effect, especially after the "Digression on Madness," is a debasement of values that previous portions of the *Tale* have upheld.

But while Swift urges the reader toward the ultimate authority of the real author, he also expands the rhetorical roles of narrator and narratee, making them enact a multitude of relationships between reader and author, ranging from complicity through contempt. In analogy to people who attempt to understand the "Vehicles of Types and Fables" that are characteristic of the "Grubean Sages," the reader of the *Tale* is in danger of being so engrossed "with the outward Lustre, as neither to regard or consider, the Person or the Parts of the Owner within" (p. 66). Even in the "Apology" Swift stages a performance that maintains, as much as it dissipates, the *Tale*'s sense of authorial evasiveness. Among the many other contentions and ambiguous assertions, Swift's remark that the three oratorial machines had been four is patently implausible, as is his remark that the original had "not so many Chasms as appear in the Book" (p. 17). Swift's explanations that the book is ironical and parodical, and that it attacks abuses "such as all Church of England Men agree in" (p. 8), are legitimate defenses against Wotton's assertion that the author is lewd and irreligious when speaking in his own person. But without questioning the serious intent of this defense, we may note that in the "Preface" Swift tends in general more to remove himself from the *Tale* than to define the positions taken in it. Although Swift complains that "Interpretations which never once entered into the Writer's Head" have been forced on the book (p. 12), he concludes the "Apology" by disclaiming any responsibility for the explanatory notes that he himself added. And having already announced that the authorship of the book is a secret from all but his closest friends, he concludes with a "Postscript" that offers to print on the title page the name of any person who can claim three lines in the whole book.

Swift's text demands that we question the relationship of narrator to author and that we find any resolution of the question to be difficult. When the assumed complicity of author and narrator is succeeded by a sharp division between them, the author's integrity as well as the narrator's is called into question. It is common, of course, for narrators to change during a work. Some rationalized alteration of a character leaves the authorial position stable. In a form that purports to be polemical, however, as satire does, such a change appears to undermine the validity of the position stated or implied before or after the change. To state the matter another way, the integrity of the work's form is questioned: Has the work been begun as one form and ended as another?

One of the most prominent satiric techniques of the *Tale* is parody, a form that allows Swift to exploit the ambiguities of the authorial position. Satiric parody distinguishes itself from foolish imitation or repetition by evoking a double vision—the narrow one that it imitates and the larger one that judges the imitation. This larger vision, which makes the parody something other than imitation or repetition, must be located in some consciousness. We sometimes speak of "self-parody," implying that someone's actions or words are both characteristic and deficient in some obvious respect. The consciousness of the parody is then located only in the observer or reader, not in the performer. Literary satire implies, however, that this consciousness is located in an author. It is, of course, sometimes difficult to tell whether authors wish us to perceive a discrepancy between a work's reality and its pretensions or whether they are merely unsuccessful in concealing that discrepancy.

One way in which authors signify the doubleness of their consciousness is by a direct entrance into the text. Authors may announce their satiric points—or they may announce themselves as the fools who wrote the subsequent foolishness. In the latter case, of course, we take the dramatized foolish "author" as an indication of the real author's consciousness of the text's limitations. But the narrator of Swift's *Tale* discusses his authorial role explicitly and foolishly while also making his satiric judgments on modern failings evident and persuasive.

Parody always has a disconcerting propensity to become very like the thing parodied (as is true of any mimetic satire: the more precisely the work defines evil, the more nearly that evil is exemplified). What begins as attack is in danger of ending as the sincerest form of flattery. The narrator of the *Tale* notices this metamorphosis when he describes those critics who constantly seek writers' faults: "Their Imaginations are so entirely possess'd and replete with the Defects of other Pens, that the very Quintessence of what is bad, does of necessity distill into their own: by which means the Whole appears to be nothing else but an *Abstract* of the *Criticisms* themselves have made" (pp. 95–96). *A Tale of a Tub* is by its own definition a modern book except insofar as it implies or represents a consciousness that discriminates between the mimed characteristics of other books and the differently intended uses of these repetitions within itself. It is to some degree shaped by what it defines as modern forms, whatever its putative or real author thinks of them. When the story of the three brothers is halted to give information that "in Method" ought to have been given previously, the narrator's attribution of this failure to the "true *Modern*" deficiency of memory does not change the sequence of the narration (pp. 134–35). When modern self-praise is parodied in the text rather than confined to a preface, "it makes a very considerable Addition to the Bulk of the Volume, *a circumstance by no means to be neglected by a skilful Writer*" (p. 132). Although the very next digression—"A Digression in Praise of Digressions"—mocks this practice of increasing bulk without any comparable increases in substance, the increase of bulk remains despite the mockery. As the satiric object and the satire accumulate more resemblances to each other, we become less certain that a consciousness manifested in the text is distinguishing between the two. The work that Swift's narrator has devised comes to resemble more and more closely the ass that he aims to satirize.

The *Tale* analyzes the dissolution of the distinction between satiric parody and foolish imitation. Fearing the true critic, the ancients at first represented their opinion of him under the hieroglyph of an ass but "were forced to leave off the use of the former *Hieroglyph,* as too nearly approaching the *Prototype*" (p. 99). Jack too resembles an ass so closely that it is difficult to distinguish "between the *Original* and the *Copy*" (p. 195). When satiric object and image finally become indistinguishable, the satire collapses. The satiric force of a comparison is derived from the consciousness of a resemblance between things of different value. When this disparity disappears, the ensuing representation is not satiric, however ignoble it is. A near resemblance of an ignoble object to one that has been presumed to be much nobler intensifies the satire, but only as long as at least a hypothetical distinction between the two is marked in some consciousness.

Rather than resisting the inevitable pressure that brings satiric image and object closer to each other, the narrator succumbs to it in the "Digression on Madness." Instead of maintaining the dual consciousness implied by his earlier narration, he rationalizes a narrowed and otiose view. He questions the basis for his and our value judgments, arguing that what we despise is on closer examination similar to what we admire: "The very same Principle that influences a *Bully* to break the windows of a Whore, who has jilted him, naturally stirs up a Great Prince to raise mightly Armies, and dream nothing but Sieges, Battles, and Victories" (p. 165). Serious moral judgments are pointless, because different actions will have the same internal sources. Furthermore, similar actions will have different meanings because of circumstances external to the actor: a man may "pass for a *Fool* in one Company" and "be treated as a Philosopher" in another (p. 168); Empedocles and Curtius each leaped into a "gulph," but one is called mad and the other the "Saver of his Country" (p. 175). Although the term "madness" implies something that we abominate, the narrator uses the word only because "the Narrowness of our Mother-tongue has not yet assigned any other name" (p. 167), not because he accepts the implicit prejudice. A philosopher is called mad and is imprisoned only because of the "Skill" or "Luck" with which he strikes a "Pitch," not because of the substance of his doctrines. Because men follow others from a "secret necessary Sympathy," praise or blame is pointless.

The narrator's analysis of the achievements of conquerors, philosophers, and religious fanatics is obviously knowing satire, but he also attacks the standpoint from which these figures are judged, drawing the conclusion that satire should be abandoned: if success is a matter of striking the right note, only pleasing fictions should be created. In his dreary world, the only happiness is delusion: "Imagination can build nobler Scenes, and produce more wonderful Revolutions than Fortune or nature will be at Expence to furnish....how shrunk is every Thing, as it appears in the Glass of Nature? So, that if it were not for the Assistance of Artificial *Mediums,* false Lights, refracted Angles, Varnish, and Tinsel; there would be a mighty Level in the Felicity and Enjoyment of Mortal Man" (p. 172). This desire for relief from the world of nature leads people to prefer madness to sanity and removes the justification for satire.

The narrator places himself in the position not of the deluded but of the one who recommends delusion, informing us that the outside is "infinitely preferable to the *In*" (p. 173). He himself has already performed the satiric anatomies necessary to demonstrate the truism that, both morally and physically, man's appearance is better than his reality (pp. 173–74). Reason tells us so, and for reason to demonstrate and redemonstrate it is officious (p. 173). He recommends that we "patch up the Flaws and Imperfections of Nature" (p. 174) rather than memorialize them; in his unpleasant world, the only "Felicity" is in achieving "The Serene Peaceful State of being a Fool among Knaves" (p. 174).

From the narrator's perspective, "The Digression on Madness" appears to convert the hermeneutical issues of the *Tale* into rhetorical ones: the discovery of meaning is subordinated to ascertaining response. But from the reader's perspective, the work moves from the commentary on external follies to a focus on the consciousness that originates this commentary, from diegesis to mimesis.[2] When the narrator attempts to abolish the distinction between his ironical and literal meanings—an attempted suppression of a part of his consciousness—his ambiguous relation to his commentary becomes the focus of attention. He has severed "intention" from its embodiment in a particular text, making "intention" stand only for his naked will. Consequently, he has also turned the "literal" into a malleable texture that, he hopes, can respond to his evanescent will rather than exemplify a fixed meaning.

In extended fictions, irony is often conceived as the narrowness of a character's vision as revealed by the more inclusive vision shared by author and reader. Martin Price, for example, remarks, "In his ironic works [Swift] creates a series of speakers, each of them unaware of one term of a possible antithesis and all the more unguarded, because of his obtuseness, in calling attention to what he disregards."[3] And Ronald Paulson sets the private language of Swift's tale-teller against "the sovereignty of the word": "When meaning splits like this and there are two levels of awareness apparent, that of the speaker and that of the reader, language has reasserted its right as sign over the Hack's employment of it as symbol."[4] The user of ironical language, however—in this case, the tale-teller—may be accorded an awareness of irony that is not necessarily any less complex than our own. Irony is a simultaneous awareness of contrarieties by a single consciousness and does not necessarily also require the representation of a singularly otiose perspective. Those readers who wish to call the tale-teller "Swift" have some such conception. If the narrator is not represented as otiose, as a purveyor of only one of the two strands necessary for irony, there is in these readers' view no point in distinguishing him from Swift. Gardner Stout, for example, following Ehrenpreis, finds that "the *Tale*'s rhetoric generally

[2]Seymour Chatman, *Story and Discourse: Narrative Structure in Fiction and Film* (Ithaca: Cornell University Press, 1978), 146, uses these terms, relating them to their source in Plato and citing their revival by Gérard Genette.

[3]Martin Price, *Swift's Rhetorical Art: A Study in Structure and Meaning* (New Haven: Yale University Press, 1953), 57.

[4]Ronald Paulson, *Theme and Structure in Swift's "Tale of a Tub"* (New Haven: Yale University Press, 1960), 52.

suggests an image of Swift, sitting with his fellow wits in an Augustan drawing room and saying: a Wotton, a Bentley, a bookseller, a hack, a Rosicrucian *adeptus* talks thus—and then striking a pose and personating them, while simultaneously carrying on an ironic (often sarcastic) running commentary on their absurdities."[5]

These two views on how irony is created in Swift are not so much differing interpretations of a text as differing conventions for analyzing irony. The first is a characteristic method for explaining irony in narrative, the second a characteristic way of doing so in polemic. The first method makes of the narrator a character in a tale that defines him; the second makes of the narrator an authorial figure who defines the tale. It is often difficult to argue that either method represents a literal approach to a given satire, especially a short one. In *A Modest Proposal*, for example, the narrator appears to make directly ironic remarks: "*I Grant* this Food will be somewhat dear, and therefore very *proper for Landlords*; who, as they have already devoured most of the Parents, seem to have the best Title to the Children" (12:112). It is implausible to deny any perpetrator of this sentence knowledge of its ironic import; nevertheless the reader's construction of even so obtuse a figure is not inconsistent with a kind of otiosity that figures elsewhere in the *Proposal*'s irony. In other passages it is difficult to comprehend what ironies Swift might be speaking directly. Many details of the proposal have no specifically polemical purpose except as part of a horrific, or comic, fantasy, and the last sentence seems designed to set the narrator apart from Swift: "I have no Children, by which I can propose to get a single Penny; the youngest being nine Years old, and my Wife past Child-bearing" (12:118). The choice of method for analyzing the irony depends usually on whether the interpreter wishes to emphasize the narrative or polemical aspects of a satire.

When the shift from hermeneutics to rhetoric, and from diegesis to mimesis, occurs in the *Tale*, two versions of the work's rhetoric and, more narrowly, of its irony are presented.

[5]Gardner Stout, "Speaker and Satiric Vision in Swift's *Tale of a Tub*," *Eighteenth Century Studies* 3 (1969), 183.

Irony does not merely become a symptom of the shared state of superiority of author and reader but is itself scrutinized. When the satiric commentator—the tale-teller—is transformed into a character, his irony reveals its own circumscriptions: this simulated author's authority is examined and is found not to be absolute. One ironic model (the simultaneous containment of an otiose and a perceptive viewpoint within the narrator) turns into another (the narrator appears otiose when scrutinized in a new context). Our interpretive choices are then revealed to entail a view of self and consciousness.

Making use of Baudelaire's *De l'essence du rire,* Paul de Man has outlined a genesis of irony and has defined certain of its potentialities in a way that is relevant to the condition that Swift examines in *A Tale of a Tub.*[6] In this view, irony is a consciousness that arises from the perception of two kinds of difference: that between oneself and others (intersubjective) and that between oneself and objects. Intersubjective differences are perceived "in terms of the superiority of one subject over another, with all of the implications of will to power, of violence, and possession which come to play when a person is laughing at someone else—including the will to educate and to improve." "The activity of a consciousness by which a man differentiates himself from the non-human world," however, is not appropriately a perception of superiority. The differentiation of oneself from things occurs in language and "transforms the *self* out of the empirical world into a world constituted out of and in language" (pp. 195–96). Falling, people can laugh at themselves, because they are reminded "of the purely instrumental reified character of. . .[the] relationship to nature." Nevertheless, being split "into an empirical self that exists in a state of inauthenticity and a self that exists only in the form of a language that asserts the knowledge of this inauthenticity" cannot give comfort, "for to know inauthenticity is not the same as to be authentic." Indeed, rather than bolstering self, the irony that

[6]Paul de Man, "The Rhetoric of Temporality," in *Interpretation: Theory and Practice,* ed. Charles S. Singleton (Baltimore: Johns Hopkins University Press, 1969), 173–209. The discussion of irony to which I refer directly here occurs on pp. 194–201.

results when we sense that our feelings of superiority to nature are inappropriate (intrasubjective irony) unravels self: "The moment the innocence or authenticity of our sense of being in the world is put into question, a far from harmless process gets under way....before long the entire texture of the self is unravelled"(p. 197).

At a climactic point in the "Digression on Madness," the narrator announces: "This is the sublime and refined Point of Felicity, called, *the Possession of being well-deceived;* The Serene Peaceful State of being a Fool among Knaves" (p. 174). The deception advocated is self-perceived self-deception. The narrator has been displaying a split self for us: the self who writes a modern book is viewed by a self who perceives the fallacies of the enterprise. Nevertheless, the enlightenment that presumably develops from the superiority of one version of the self to the other is eventually superseded by the sense of the inauthenticity of the superior self. The goals and literary procedures of both selves are linked, and even the value system that makes one superior to the other is suspect. The narrator sees his own implication in the system that he has used to reduce the moderns to mechanisms: not only their achievement but also his begins with mere vapors, and his own book is derived from the books of others. What began as a method for controlling externalities—literalizing and materializing—becomes a metaphor of self-perception. Rather than avoiding this perception, he iterates it and attempts to suppress his irony. Seeking refuge in a literary self, he argues that withdrawal into pleasing fictions is justified by the painfulness of our empirical world. Although the concluding segments continue the themes of the earlier portions of the work, they are increasingly disoriented by the narrator's inability to authenticate any perspective from which to deliver his words.

Swift's dramatization of his narrator's inauthentic relationships to his chosen literary form implies that the form has a meaning independent of the narrator's use of it. The narrator is constrained by the form even as he abuses it. Many of the cruxes of interpretation of Swift's *Tale* result from its manipulation of an already complex form—the mock encomium of the moderns—to the end of revealing the self-aggrandizing "author" hiding in the role of detached and witty satirist. Swift found in Montaigne the analysis of subjectivity that formed his treatment of the narrator in the *Tale;* in his *Essays,* Montaigne subdued to self a series of announced external subjects. Swift's narrator attempts to subdue both a lengthy narrative and a complex literary form.

The formal model for Swift's *Tale* is Erasmus's *Moriae encomium (The Praise of Folly).* In this work, Erasmus explores the divergences between a form and its narrator, or more descriptively, its performer. Erasmus's work is a variation on the mock encomium—a satiric form that blames by means of inappropriate praise—and Swift's work is an extension of Erasmus's method. In *Praisers of Folly,* Walter Kaiser shows that Erasmus's *Praise of Folly* was a departure from the methods of previous mock encomiums: "What would have been astonishing to the reader of 1511 . . . is the fact that here the ridiculous is praising itself."[7] The title may be read either as "the praise spoken by Folly" or as "Folly praised." As Kaiser suggests, it means both: "Folly's Praise of Folly." But this kind of mock encomium is, again in Kaiser's words, "a vertiginous semantic labyrinth": "Erasmus' book is a mock encomium but at the same time the mocking is mocked. I know of no other mock encomium before the *Moriae encomium* that employs this subtle device, and after Erasmus only Swift successfully approximates it." Any praise of an apparently unsuitable object suggests paradox, but these works of Swift and Erasmus especially warrant their designation as "paradoxical mock encomiums." While praising obviously unworthy things, both works also question the values that define these praised things as obviously unworthy. They exemplify abundantly the "profoundly self-critical . . . comment on their own method and their own technique" that Rosalie Colie sees as characteristic of all paradoxes.[8]

[7]Walter Kaiser, *Praisers of Folly* (Cambridge: Harvard University Press, 1963), 36. Subsequent quotations of Kaiser in this paragraph are from pp. 36 and 37 of his book.

[8]Rosalie Colie, *Paradoxia Epidemica: The Renaissance Tradition of Paradox*

Erasmus's Folly and Swift's tale-teller are organized by their adopted roles as narrators of mock encomiums, forms that present themselves as rhetorical exercises with the aim of making plausible what is absurd. Finally, we may find much of serious import in the form, but initially it seems a game whose goal is to defend the indefensible, a defiance of the credible. The narrators of such forms are necessarily, at least initially, sophists whose personal beliefs are less in question than their abilities to sustain the semblance of an argument that will interest and amuse us. The argument requires only enough reason to keep it from collapsing, and the arguer does not fail as long as he (or she) can keep it going to a determinate end. Of course, the author may have in mind some greater ironic truth, but the author's end is ordinarily achieved not by our acceptance of the sophistic arguments but by our acknowledgment of a dimension to reality not fully accounted for in our more nearly rational versions of truth.[9]

In the following analysis of Erasmus's work, I attempt to isolate several elements that are comparable to elements of Swift's *Tale*. I am especially concerned with Folly's consciousness of her own performance and with the manner in which the contradictions of her performance expose a contrary view.

Erasmus's Folly makes few attempts to conceal her sophis-

(Princeton: Princeton University Press, 1966), 7. Henry Knight Miller, "The Paradoxical Encomium with Special Reference to Its Vogue in England, 1600-1800," *Modern Philology* 53 (1956), 145-78, defines the mock encomium, establishes its vogue in England in the period that he discusses, and provides a list of examples. Miller attributes a portion of the English interest in the form to translations of Erasmus's book (p. 155). Ronald Paulson, *Theme and Structure in Swift's "Tale of a Tub,"* defines a considerable number of the parallels between the *Tale* and the *Praise of Folly* (see especially pp. 79-80, 249-53) but identifies Folly's perspective with Erasmus's much more closely than I think appropriate (pp. 136, 249).

[9]Rosalie Colie, *Paradoxia Epidemica,* explains the rhetorical paradox as "an ancient form designed...to show off the skill of an orator and to arouse the admiration of an audience, both at the outlandishness of the subject and the technical brilliance of the rhetorician" (p. 3). John R. Clark, *Form and Frenzy in Swift's "Tale of a Tub"* (Ithaca: Cornell University Press, 1970), discusses the background of paradox and comments extensively on the paradoxical sayings of Swift's modern (pp. 181-230).

tries but ingratiates her folly and its bad repute by her wit. She makes her self-praise a jest, not an embarrassment: "What can be more proper than that Folly be her own trumpet? For who can set me out better than myself. . .?"[10] She engages attention by her assaults on logic and the cleverness of her strategems. But as she undermines the pretenses of wisdom, the small truths that she entraps in her equivocations loom large.

Folly accepts any kind of pleasure as the goal of life, a position sometimes vulgarly associated with Epicureanism but not one espoused by Erasmus. In his colloquy "The Epicurean," Erasmus defines the nature of Christian pleasure and distinguishes his version of Epicureanism from the vulgar version. Cicero's *De finibus bonorum et malorum,* a work alluded to in the colloquy, may have suggested to Erasmus the idea of making Folly a debased Epicurean equivocator. One of Cicero's central criticisms of Epicurus is that he lacks "the whole armour of Logic": "He does away with Definition; he has no doctrine of Division or Partition; he gives no rules for Deduction or Syllogistic Inference, and imparts no method for resolving Dilemmas or for detecting Fallacies of Equivocation" (see Folly's announcement of her oratorical practices below).[11] And Cicero specifically accuses his Epicurean opponents of using the term "pleasure" in varying senses (Cicero, pp. 83, 85).

Folly begins her oration by establishing an identity between herself and her chosen form and theme—the praise of foolishness. She recreates the world in her own image—pleasant, sensual, amoral, irresponsible—and argues that our social structures would collapse without her pleasing illusions. Folly is also an imperialist, however: she has "erected an empire over emperors themselves" and desires to be the *"alpha,* or first, of all the gods" (p. 15). Her oration is itself the establishment of this kingdom. She encompasses by equivocation, giv-

[10]Desiderius Erasmus, *The Praise of Folly,* trans. John Wilson, 1668 (Ann Arbor: University of Michigan Press, 1958), 3. Subsequent references will be to this translation, which contains one of the several uses of the phrase "Tale of a Tub" shortly before Swift's use of it.

[11]Cicero, *De finibus,* ed. and trans. H. Rackham, Loeb Classical Library (London: William Heineman, 1914), 25; *The Colloquies of Erasmus,* trans. Craig R. Thompson (Chicago: University of Chicago Press, 1965).

ing multiple meanings to madness and folly, and rejecting even
the rhetorical methods of definition and division because they
imply limitation (p. 10). This urge toward expansion, however,
makes her claim subjects whom she recognizes to be repulsive.
Erasmus then creates a disjunction between Folly as a person-
age and as a personality. As she enlists the vicious and destructive among her followers, she is besmirched by her
manifestations. Her kingdom divides against itself—folly as destructiveness against folly as a palliative of destructiveness—
and her sophistic praise becomes openly satiric. But despite her
understanding that many of her followers are despicable, Folly
dissociates herself from satire: "But it is not my business to sift
too narrowly the lives of prelates and priests for fear I seem to
have intended rather a satire than an oration" (p. 124). Folly
unmasks folly in order to claim and domesticate it, not to eradi-
cate it.

Folly's espousal of Christianity shows her betrayal by the
mock encomium that she uses to create her dominion. She
praises Christianity because it is from her perspective an ex-
traordinarily foolish rejection of all that she assumes to be valuable. But if accepted, it would destroy the foundations of her
world: "It would bring in watchings, fastings, tears, prayers,
sermons, good endeavors, sighs, and a thousand the like trou-
blesome exercises" (p. 119). In her enthusiasm for expanding
the kingdom of folly, she has praised a truth that fatally divides
it against itself. Hastily she breaks off her discourse, asking that
her auditors not remember her words or at least not take them
seriously: "But I forget myself and run beyond my
bounds....I hate a man that remembers what he hears.
Wherefore farewell, clap your hands, live and drink lustily, my
most excellent disciples of Folly" (p. 152). As Erasmus remarks
in his "Preface" to More, "having brought her in speaking, it
was but fit that I kept up the character of her person" (p. 5).
Folly's praise of Christianity, given her premises, is a mistake,
not a conversion.[12]

[12]Walter Kaiser, in *Praisers of Folly*, writes that "Erasmus' legacy to European thought was more than a formal stylistic one....it is, in the last analysis, Stultitia herself...who casts her shadow across the subsequent ages"

In his "Preface," Swift's tale-teller defines himself as a panegyrist, at the same time comparing panegyric and satire (pp. 49–53). Panegyric is more difficult to write than satire, he argues, because the "Follies and Vices" of people are more abundant than their virtues (p. 50). As the narrator's very discussion of panegyric is satire, he places his work securely within the tradition of the mock encomium. Later in the digressions, Swift's tale-teller praises modern accomplishments in a way that emphasizes their deficiencies, and in the tale, he applauds the obviously disreputable Aeolists and Jack.

The rhetorical stance of Folly and that of the tale-teller differ, however. Folly is aware that praise of folly, especially by Folly, is risible, and she assumes that there is an inherent satirical tendency in her form. Her goal is to mitigate the satire, however—to show an attractive geniality in the apparent satiric objects. Her mordant and direct satire emerges only when she exposes the folly hidden in the pretenses of wisdom. She is then driven to attack her enemies in order to claim them. Swift's tale-teller too is aware that the objects of his praise are in some respects indefensible. And like Folly, he assumes that his form is a not entirely serious rhetorical exercise. But Swift's narrator satirizes more sharply and directly than Folly does; unlike Folly, he is without an allegorical identification with his subject matter.[13]

Because Swift's narrator has a role less precisely defined than that of Erasmus's Folly, he has fewer restrictions on his topic. His generalized desire to be "quit of number" imposes no theme on him. While his chosen method of succeeding is to

---

(p. 92). There has not, however, been agreement about what Folly means. Kaiser, e.g., argues that Folly encompasses the meanings of the book, that she asks us at the end to applaud her and also "to live the Christian life she has extolled" (p. 90). But Rosalie Colie, in *Paradoxia Epidemica,* remarks that Folly "has abandoned the reader to make his own decisions about value" (p. 20).

[13]Discussion of the *Tale*'s narrator is difficult because the words of the *Tale* are not easily reconciled to a conception of their narrator either as stupid or as Swift. As Edward Rosenheim, in *Swift and the Satirist's Art* (Chicago: University of Chicago Press, 1963), argues, the narrator's "outrageous mock-logical excursions can rest on a foundation of brutal truth" (p. 142).

write a book, his identity as an author is unrestricted. He has the freedom to construct or reconstruct himself; no self-definition is denied to him. He wants to be nothing that will inhibit success and anything that will contribute to his advancement. It does not matter that his arguments are openly sophistical, but it does matter that they are clever and amusing. He has chosen to exalt himself by writing, and he attempts to focus attention on the writing, not on some ulterior issue. The wit to exploit absurdity is more important than some logic of continuity; content is an obstacle to be overcome. This rationalized divergence between a given form and its executor implies a self that exists independently of the form although revealed in it.

In both Swift's *Tale* and Erasmus's *Praise of Folly*, the mock encomium is disrupted. Before the "Digression on Madness," the praise of the moderns has been an amusing, if tart, exercise in illogicality. Moderns are aberrants who are condescendingly praised and sneered at by the narrator. But in the "Digression on Madness," the narrator subsumes many of man's achievements under the various categories of madness. The mad moderns become, then, not just an aberration in man's history but a dominant group; consequently the narrator's tone of superiority is modified by his sense of their sinister force. This digression turns Swift's *Tale* into a darker work than Erasmus's *Praise of Folly*. Folly finally praises the Christianity that deserves to be substituted for the foolishness that she has been praising. She inadvertently shows us an alternative to her views, but the tale-teller praises something that justifies the foolishness that he has been exhibiting. Erasmus presents a saving seriousness in Folly's equivocation, and Swift presents the consequences of rejecting that saving seriousness.

The question of whether or not we must read the early parts of the text in a different way after the exposure of the narrator in the "Digression on Madness" implies that we have a choice. We necessarily read both ways, however—in accord with the form and then in accord with its collapse. All along the narrator has been clownish and abrasive. Nevertheless, the mock encomium allows an argument to be conducted without requiring its narrator to assume full responsibility for it. The loosened logic and the paradoxes that are characteristic of the form prevent us from categorizing the narrator as an object of satire. Still, the limitations of Swift's narrator are organized and formulated after this pivotal digression and his subsequent disintegration. Then the separation of self from performance clearly exposes tensions that have been implicit all along.

From the beginning, Swift has given us the hints that are eventually formulated. The tale-teller, like Folly, is obviously attempting to dominate by means of his words. The very combination on the title page of what Wotton called the gibberish of "Marcosian Hereticks" (p. 30) with the lofty ambitions of Lucretius identifies, as it mocks, the putative author's grandiose pretensions to the authority of poet and prophet. The tale-teller is much more aggressive than Folly, who by her naming is given a role. She must elucidate and expand her role, but she can rest secure in her position as a great goddess, even if her ambitions remain incompletely realized. But the tale-teller's differing situation is announced in a statement that Edward Rosenheim calls "a kind of leitmotif for the entire *Tale*": "Whoever hath an Ambition to be heard in a Crowd, must press, and squeeze, and thrust, and climb with indefatigable Pains, till he has exalted himself to a certain Degree of Altitude above them" (p. 55).[14] He is aware that literary forms establish an author's relationship to his audience, speculating that the ancients used panegyric and satire to "soften, or divert the Censorious Reader" (p. 97). And in the "Introduction," he explains his views of the effects of the two forms, altering the usual relationship: panegyric arouses hostile envy in its readers but satire creates a comfortable sense of its readers' superiority (p. 51). Even his ironic comparison of the literary forms is self-praise: he, unlike most moderns, writes a more difficult form than satire, "the Materials of Panegyrick being very few in Number" (p. 49). Although this remark is satiric in itself, he uses his witty satire as the foundation of his self-praise, the platform by which he elevates himself above the crowd.

[14]Rosenheim, *Swift and the Satirist's Art*, 69.

The narrator's fate is finally to be convinced by his own sophistry, believing that success in the ways of the world is the ultimate goal of all activity and that the ways of the world are madness. But two aspects of his performance prior to the "Digression on Madness" are not easily defined as symptoms of his folly: one is the sustained brilliance of his attack on the moderns, and the other is the apparent serious meaning of the allegory of the three brothers. Nevertheless, even these aspects of the *Tale* include symptoms that link them to the later aspects of the *Tale*.

Swift devises a stylistic contrast between the "Preface" and the two adjacent portions of the Tale, the preceding "Dedication" and the subsequent "Introduction." The voice of the narrator enters the *Tale* with "The Epistle Dedicatory, to His Royal Highness Prince Posterity." This dedicatee is fantastical and inappropriate to the bookseller's mundane purposes (p. 22), but the dedication is a brilliant tour de force of parody and paradoxical logic, an ingenious rhetorical exercise that praises modern books until they are roundly condemned. The narrator begins, as Swift's note remarks, "by personating other writers, who sometimes offer such Reasons and Excuses for publishing their Works as they ought chiefly to conceal and be asham'd of" (p. 30). He then argues, denigrating as he praises, that despite Time's malice, his fellow modern authors do survive, that is, as paper, although he does not wish to send Posterity "for ocular conviction to a *Jakes,* or an *Oven*; to the Windows of a Bawdy-house, or to a sordid *Lanthorn*" (p. 36). The following section, the "Preface," is, like the "Dedication," a knowing catalog of modern deficiencies, but it is a less polished performance. Its movement is abrupt, as the narrator twice notes: "But, to return" (p. 42); "But I forget" (p. 53). Occasionally the intended urbanity of blame by praise becomes invective, as in his remarks on satirists: "Most of our late Satyrists seem to lye under a sort of Mistake, that because Nettles have the Prerogative to Sting; therefore all *other Weeds* must do so too" (p. 48). The account of the purpose of the book at the beginning of the "Preface"—"to employ those unquiet Spirits" (p. 41)—establishes a sense of the narrator's amused superiority, but

79

these following vacillations of tone suggest instead a sense of barely controlled tensions.

The subsequent "Introduction" is controlled and confident, as forceful and exact as the dedication and with little of the vacillation that appeared in the "Preface." Here the narrator defines three methods of rising—pulpit, ladder, stage itinerant—wittily exploiting the disreputable aspects of each and seeming to wander far from any apparent consistency of subject. But he then demonstrates that his wit is equal to the task of bringing all within the compass of his purpose: "Now this Physico-logical Scheme of Oratorial Receptacles or Machines, contains a great Mystery, being a Type, a Sign, an Emblem, a Shadow, a Symbol, bearing Analogy to the spacious Commonwealth of Writers, and to those Methods by which they must exalt themselves to a certain Eminency above the inferiour World" (p. 61).

The fiction explaining this contrast between the unsettled "Preface" and its adjacent sections is defined in the "Preface" itself; this portion of the work has been written after the remainder had been completed: "Thrice Have I forced my Imagination to make the *Tour* of my Invention, and thrice it has returned empty; the latter having been totally drained by the following Treatise" (p. 42). The state of mind reflected in the "Preface" is that toward which the work tends: the reader is given a hint that the early controlled narration is the beginning stage of a process leading to confusion and exhaustion.

The other seemingly reputable part of the narrator's performance is the story of the three brothers, which appears to have a weight of seriousness that is able to counterbalance the narrator's egoism until late in the *Tale*. Still, the seemingly sharp separations of the foolish digressions from the serious story are more evident in appearance than in reality. The tale-teller attempts to exploit the Horatian admonition that "the Publick Good of Mankind is performed by two Ways, *Instruction* and *Diversion*" (p. 124). Although he regards his digressions as the sweetness that will make the instruction palatable, he also calls attention to his reworking of the three brothers' story because he is not confident that the reader's interest will be sustained by the instruction. The story is not the narrator's, but he reshapes it rather than merely transcribing it: "Here the Story says, this good Father died....I shall not trouble you with recounting what Adventures they met" (p. 74). The narrator has a sense of story patterns that enables him to slide easily through unnecessary detail and also to embellish opportunely. Recognizing a too-familiar romance pattern, he rounds off the story jocularly: "They travelled thro' several Countries, encountred a reasonable Quantity of Gyants, and slew certain Dragons" (p. 74). He provides an energetic summary of their viciousness in town (pp. 74–75) but ceases when their "Qualifications" in the ways of the world finally become "too tedious to recount" (p. 75).

The next portion of this installment of the tale deals with the clothes philosophy (pp. 75–81), which is not just the narrator's reworking of the story but his contribution to it: "with much Pains and Reading" he has collected the "short Summary of a Body of Philosophy and Divinity" (p. 80) that is essential to understanding the story of the brothers. He pretends, thinly, that it is a historical account, but it is obviously a satiric allegory grounded in Hobbesian materialism. The narrative is absurd but clever, an exercise of the narrator's gift of irreverent satire: "Is not Religion a cloak...and Conscience a *Pair of Breeches,* which tho' a Cover for Lewdness as well as Nastiness, is easily slipt down for the Service of both" (p. 78).

This interpolation by the narrator shapes the remainder of the tale's first installment. A lady is reported to have cried out at one of the brothers, "That Fellow...has no Soul; where is his Shoulder-knot?" (p. 82). The language of Peter, as well as of the narrator, assumes the tone of scholarly erudition appropriate to the narrator's interpolated philosophical discourse but absent from the earlier portion of the tale: "You are to be informed, that, of wills *duo sunt genera,* Nuncupatory and scriptory" (p. 85). Like the narrator, Peter too develops a skill in allegorical interpretation.

The subsequent sections of the story of the three brothers, sections 4 and 6, call attention to the narrator even more insistently than the opening section does. Section 4 begins, "I have now with much Pains and Study conducted the Reader" (p. 105); and later paragraphs of this section refer to his hopes that his story will find translators (p. 106) and commentators (p. 114). In section 4 the narrator remarks directly on the brothers as characters of his creation, even though he follows a history: "The generous Author...finds his Hero on the Dunghil, from thence by gradual Steps, raises Him to a Throne, and then immediately withdraws...in imitation of which Example, I have placed *Lord Peter* in a Noble House, given Him a Title to wear, and Money to spend" (p. 133). And this section is later interrupted by the narrator's reference to his "excellent *Analytical* Discourse upon" zeal (p. 137). The first of these sections (4) is a satire on Peter and the next (6) on Jack: the narrator is not deceived about either. His aim, however, is not to present their story forcefully but to present himself. In the first installment of their story, he carefully shapes the narrative material to elicit admiration for his authorial abilities, and in subsequent sections he presents his self-advertisements directly. His pretenses of subtlety vanish as he more insistently demands praise.

Section 8 (on the Aeolists) is presented as another installment of the story of the three brothers, but, like the clothes philosophy, it is material collected and developed by the narrator to add a dimension required for comprehending the story of the brothers. And again, like the narrator's previous interpolation, it is satire written from a Hobbesian perspective. Aeolism is connected to the story line because it is a satire of Jack and his Presbyterian followers: "Into this *Barrel,* upon Solemn Days, the Priest enters; where...a secret Funnel is also convey'd from his Posteriors, to the Bottom of the Barrel, which admits new Supplies of Inspiration from a *Northern* Chink or Crany" (p. 156). The narrator does not continue his comment on Jack in specific terms, however, but puts him into historical perspective, noting that his patterns of behavior ally him to similar aberrations throughout the ages.

The sections on Aeolism and Madness (8 and 9) are not clearly either story or digression (the section on madness continues the exploration of the success of Jack, an Aeolist), and in the succeeding sections the narrator is unable to recover the distinction. Of the three sections following the "Digression on Madness," only section II deals directly with the story of the three brothers, and substantial portions of that section are digressive. As Jay Arnold Levine describes this aspect of the *Tale*, "the religious allegory, or Bible, breaks down under the pressure of the disordered personality that, as the *Tale* proceeds, escapes from the confinement of the digressions and captures the entire work."[15]

Even the seemingly sharp disjunctions between digressions and tale in the earlier portions of the work are balanced by thematic continuities. Section 2 ends with the brothers' elaborate misinterpretations of the will, and section 3 is the digression on critics. In section 4 Peter turns projector and virtuoso, and section 5 explains the ludicrous mechanistic advances of moderns over ancients. Sections are connected not only by these obvious thematic continuities but also by repeated motifs. The clothes philosophy of the first installment of the story of the three brothers becomes the true critic as tailor in the very next section (pp. 101–102). The allegory of the critic as ass in section 3 becomes the ass's head as confessor in section 4 (pp. 107–108) and Jack as ass in section II (p. 195). The talent of moderns for deducing applications "from the *Pudenda* of either Sex" (p. 147, "Digression in Praise of Digressions") is transformed in section II (the late history of Jack) into an account of ears having an application to the pudenda (pp. 200–201). These patterns may be multiplied beyond endurance. Even the broad moral and psychological patterns of story and digression are similar. For example, the insolent irascibility by which Peter achieves his ill-deserved success is analogous to the narrator's method of rising. The similarities imply that the mind being displayed and anatomized by Swift in both story and digressions is the same: the impulse to rise to "a certain Degree of Altitude above [the crowd]" governs both strands of the *Tale*.[16]

[15]Jay Arnold Levine, "The Design of a *Tale of a Tub* (with a Digression on a Mad Modern Critic)," *ELH: A Journal of English Literary History* 33 (1966), 209.
[16]Miriam Kosh Starkman, *Swift's Satire on Learning in "A Tale of a Tub"*

The narrator's story is about the development of Christianity, as its annotations remind us. But neither Swift nor the narrator is exclusively concerned to tell us that story again. The narrative sometimes proceeds with reference to historical chronology but not consistently so. Its typology is vague and deliberately obfuscated.

What, for example, is the meaning of the allegory of the coats? William Wotton explained, not very helpfully: "By his coats which he gave his Sons, the Garments of the Israelites are exposed, which by the Miraculous Power of God waxed not old, nor were worn out for Forty years together in the Wilderness."[17] Swift gave a portion of Wotton's comment in a note to the fifth edition of the *Tale* in 1710 and followed it by a refutation signed "Lambin": "An Error (with Submission) of the learned Commentator; for by the Coats are meant the Doctrine and Faith of Christianity, by the Wisdom of the Divine founder fitted to all Times, Places and Circumstances" (p. 73). Despite Swift's mockery, Wotton does locate the rather obvious source

---

(Princeton: Princeton University Press, 1950), provides a detailed summary of connections between the allegory and the digressions (pp. 131–43). Phillip Harth, *Swift and Anglican Rationalism: The Religious Background of "A Tale of a Tub"* (Chicago: University of Chicago Press, 1961), believes that the tale and digressions are unconnected in manner, method, or subject: "*A Tale of a Tub,* then, is a satire which deals with two separate subjects, in two separate groups of sections, by means of two separate satirical methods" (p. 6). In his very favorable review of Harth's book, Ricardo Quintana remarks on the difficulties of Harth's procedure: "The *Tale* may have been worked out at different times, but its composition must be seen to include the final arrangement of the different parts into an astonishing baroque work of art, in which each part acquires significance as it plays against or with—sometimes against and with—the others" (*Modern Philology* 60 [1962–63], 143). Harold D. Kelling, "Reason in Madness: *A Tale of a Tub,*" PMLA 69 (1954), asserts that "the allegory is not written from the point of view of an Anglican clergyman, interested in demonstrating the necessity of interpreting the New Testament reasonably and applying its 'plain easy directions,' but from the point of view of a Grub-Street writer intent on proving that Jack and Peter have purposes and use methods similar to his own and are in fact, along with Wotton and the other learned moderns, members of the Grub-Street brotherhood and successful delusive orators" (p. 203).

[17]William Wotton, *Observations upon the "Tale of a Tub,"* reprinted in *A Tale of a Tub,* ed. A. C. Guthkelch and D. Nichol Smith, 2d ed. (Oxford: Clarendon Press, 1958), 317.

of the coat motif, although he does not interpret the type: "Thy raiment waxed not old upon thee, neither did thy foot swell, these forty years" (Deut. 8:4; see also Deut. 29:5; and Neh. 9:21). Swift is even responsible for resolving the rather curious problem that is raised by the biblical text alluded to by Wotton—how is bodily growth to be accommodated to the fixities of clothes: "They will grow in the same proportion with your Bodies" (p. 73). The Lambin footnote, however, interprets the type rather than merely giving its source. But closer scrutiny of the implications of the comment Swift signed "Lambin" leaves the interpretation more muddled than Wotton left it. To call the coats "the Doctrine and Faith of Christianity" is to become a clothes philosopher, to see souls in shoulder knots. It turns the doctrine and faith of Christianity into a fashion that must adapt itself to times, places, and circumstances.

Lambinus, long dead (1516–72), was an editor of classical texts who had provided the edition of Lucretius's *De rerum natura* that was standard in Swift's day, a book that Swift had read three times during the period in which he was writing the *Tale* and that was, in the edition of Lambinus, in Swift's own library. Swift used Lambinus's name in order to suggest the misplaced concreteness of the Lucretian materialism that was commonly associated with Hobbism at the time. Furthermore, he ridicules rigorous interpretations of an allegory that is just as often a reflection of the tale-teller's whims as an elucidation of Christian doctrine.

I do not mean that the story has no point but that the meaning is accessible only as it is glimpsed through the tale-teller's literary aspirations. As Ronald Paulson remarks, "These coats are a representation of an external law, the 'visible church'— that by virtue of which one is not oneself but a part of a community."[18] The story of the coats is that of the development of the *institutions* of Christianity, but for Peter and Jack the coats become more important than the will of the Father. The jostlings of Wotton and Lambinus too are a diversion from the

[18]Paulson, *Theme and Structure in Swift's "Tale of a Tub,"* 108.

moral issues of the document that they pretend to interpret: their egoistic interpolations obscure the point of the tale. The failures in Christianity that are represented by the story of the brothers are replicated in the tale-teller and in the tale's commentators. The commentators' theological interpretations, as well as the philosophical interpolations of the narrator, use the coats for purposes having little relation to the rather simple moral point observable in the outlines of the tale: the institutions of Christianity should conform to the Father's will for the purpose of representing the teaching of Christianity. Instead, the focus of concern becomes the advancement of the institutions of the church.

The narrator's early precise attack on the moderns by means of a mock encomium ends in his loss of any power over his chosen form. The movement of the book from a beginning in strength to an end in exhaustion is explained by the narrator's metaphor of bloodletting: "Since my *Vein* is once opened, I am content to exhaust it all at a Running, for the Peculiar Advantage of my dear Country, and for the universal Benefit of Mankind" (p. 184). The medical imagery of satire is conventionally of disease and a cure, both often repulsive, but this narrator remains febrile.[19] Prosecuting a traditional literary form for his own peculiar advantage, he loses control of it, becoming one with those he ought to heal.

[19]See Mary Claire Randolph, "The Medical Concept in English Renaissance Satiric Theory: Its Possible Relationships and Implications," *Studies in Philology* 38 (1941), 125–57.

CHAPTER 4

Epistemological Foundations

The metaphoric equation of a book either to a world or to a person conflates hermeneutics and epistemology. The complexities of interpreting a book are brought into relationship with larger questions about the basis of any kind of knowledge. Swift's emphasis in both the *Tale* and the *Travels* is on the limits of human knowledge, including that of the authorial figure. Swift's authors are more limited than their pretensions, unlike such vatic figures as Teiresias, Homer, or Milton, who comprehend more without eyes than we can having eyes. To generalize (perhaps grossly), writing is for Swift inevitably an expression of self. But Swift does not, like Montaigne, use this perception to sanction the pursuit of self as the most legitimate object of writing. Instead, he attempts to counteract self by attending persistently to its deforming powers. Swift's conception of self includes a recognition that the world existing beyond is at least to some degree available as a counterbalance to individual assertion. For Swift, self is a standpoint but not necessarily an enclosure.

The hermeneutical obfuscations of the *Tale* raise questions not just about the possibility that a reader can attain a valid interpretation of an author's meaning but also about the possibility that any intelligible relationship can exist with something beyond the self. Books, even wills, raise these questions, as the reader who has followed the brothers' exegetical impositions on the will and has also considered his own harried relationship to the *Tale* knows. The rhetorical issue involved is that of the tale-teller's function: Does he represent Swift's bafflement or his exemplary warning? But the more inclusive issue is epistemological. Readers who wish to find some mitigation of the tale-teller's dilemma—the materialistic version of reality to which his only alternative is delusive fictions—must do so on the basis of a more encompassing epistemology. These hermeneutical and epistemological problems are continued in the shorter works that Swift published with the *Tale of a Tub*—*The Battle of the Books*, and *A Discourse Concerning the Mechanical Operation of the Spirit*. These works too pursue the discussion of the relationship of the literal to the allegorical, the equation of books to persons, and the reduction of books to the materials of which they are made. Nevertheless these shorter satires, in combination with the *Tale*, also produce a clarified view of Swift's epistemology.

The *Battle* obviously vivifies books by means of its allegory, although the bookseller announces the contradictory view: "So, when *Virgil* is mentioned, we are not to understand the Person of a famous Poet, call'd by that Name, but only certain Sheets of Paper, bound up in Leather, containing in Print, the Works of the said Poet, and so of the rest" (*Tale*, p. 214). The allegory, of course, turns them not into volumes but into writers, with the expected range in qualities from the nasty to the sublime. Even the great Virgil exhibits a human diffidence when deceived by Dryden rather than the fixity of a book (*Tale*, p. 247).

The allegorical layers and inversions of the *Tale* are abundantly present in both the *Battle* and the *Mechanical Operation*. The *Battle* places an allegory within an allegory and stylistically disrupts the reader's assumption that one should be literal, the other figurative. The obvious allegorization of the ancients-and-moderns controversy by means of animated books is abruptly halted by the seemingly literal encroachment of a bee upon a spider's web. The earlier allegory of ancients and moderns, however, is presented in a verisimilar style: "*Plato* was by chance upon the next shelf, and observing those that spoke to be in the ragged Plight, mentioned awhile ago . . . , laugh'd aloud, and in his pleasant way, swore, *By G——, he believ'd them"* (*Tale*, p. 228). The apparently less allegorical spider is introduced in a heavily metaphoric style: "For upon the highest Corner of the large Window, there dwelt a certain *Spider*, swollen up to the first Magnitude, by the Destruction of infinite Numbers of *Flies*, whose spoils lay scattered before the Gates of his Palace, like human Bones before the Cave of some Giant" (*Tale*, p. 228). The spider and the bee show themselves to be creatures of fable when they begin to talk, and they are then turned by Aesop into an allegorical interpretation of the allegory of the ancients and moderns of which Aesop himself is a part.[1] The *Mechanical Operation* even more blatantly and perversely confounds the literal and the figurative when its narrator asserts that his narrative is an allegory of an ass: "If you please from hence forward, instead of the Term, *Ass*, we shall make use of *Gifted* or *enlightened Teacher*; And the Word *Rider*, we will exchange for that of *Fanatick Auditory*" (*Tale*, p. 265).

Given the difficulties of interpreting the *Tale*, why should these works that seemingly participate so fully in the hermeneutical confusions of the longer work give any clearer evidence of an epistemological perspective? After all, both shorter works dramatize an author who is in some ways similar to the tale-teller. The narrator of the *Battle* shares the same bumptious irascibility, and the narrator of the *Mechanical Operation* adopts the Hobbesian perspective of the clothes philosophy and the commentary on Aeolism. A crucial difference, however, is that the narrators of the shorter works do not have their positions eroded in the course of their narratives. Whether we regard either narrator as perceptive or imperceptive, involved or uninvolved, there is no shift of perspective to undermine any sta-

[1]Thomas E. Maresca, *Epic to Novel* (Columbus: Ohio State University Press, 1974), remarks that "Aesop's allegorization [in the *Battle*] only makes things more confusing; he is, after all, an allegorical figure himself, who provides us, in the middle of an allegory, with another allegory" (p. 164). On the implications of Swift's manipulations of allegory, Maresca remarks trenchantly, "His whole point lies in the tenuous connection between art and reality, between word and thing, and the myriad ways in which that connection can be broken" (p. 165).

89

ble view that the reader has constructed. Neither of these narrators is altered by his narration. In contrast, the *Tale* mimes a cycle of response in its narrator, from an initial brusque energy to a subsidence in exhaustion: the narrator's attitudes are reorganized and altered by his narration. But when the narrator of the *Mechanical Operation* imposes an irrelevant form on his material, he makes only an apparent satiric gesture that has no consequences for the development of his subsequent narration or for his conception of it. He identifies an irrelevant epistolary frame for his work at the beginning and evokes it perfunctorily at the end, but it provides no device for marking his changing relationship to the narrative, as the story-digression sequences and the variations on the praise of folly do in the *Tale*.

As compared with the *Tale*, these two shorter works place less emphasis on the authorial choices by which they come into being and more emphasis on their status as a definition of a preexisting condition in the world: their satiric aspects are less frequently subverted by their narrative aspects. The epistemological position that these shorter works imply is validated not by the narrator's recommendation or attack but by a series of images that place historical figures in contrasting relationships and imply a point of comparison. These familiar historical figures create an epistemological myth that organizes diverse kinds of error and becomes a standard for evaluation.

The general configurations of the epistemology exhibited in the *Tale of a Tub* volume coincide with a limited version of Baconian empiricism, which has as its aim (in Bacon's words) the establishing of a "true and lawful marriage between the empirical and rational faculty, the unkind and ill-starred separation of which has thrown into confusion all the affairs of the human

[2]*The Philosophical Works of Francis Bacon*, ed. John M. Robertson and based on the Spedding and Ellis text (London: George Routledge and Sons, 1905), 246. Subsequent references are to this text. Miriam Kosh Starkman, *Swift's Satire on Learning in "A Tale of a Tub"* (Princeton: Princeton University Press, 1950), 10, finds that although Swift never satirizes Bacon, he is "merciless to Baconianism." She singles out in particular those aspects of the new science that Baconians and Cartesians shared as the object of Swift's attacks (pp. 64–69). In contrast, I find that Swift separates Descartes and Bacon rather

family." ² (By the "empirical" Bacon refers to the data of experience prior to rational analysis.) The results of experiments
must be "altered and digested" in the "understanding" (Bacon, p. 288); however, "the Understanding must not therefore
be supplied with wings, but rather hung with weights to keep it
from leaping and flying" (Bacon, p. 290). Bacon's concern is
not just with the experimental method, narrowly conceived,
but with a habit of mind: "If those schoolmen in their great
thirst of truth and unwearied travail of wit had joined variety
and universality of reading and contemplation, they had
proved excellent lights, to the great advancement of all learning
and knowledge" (Bacon, p. 56). And in almost Swiftian language, Bacon suggests that there is a correlation between moral
corruption and the narrowness of learning that leads men to
"refer all things to themselves, and thrust themselves into the
centre of the world as if all lines should meet in them and their
fortunes" (Bacon, p. 52). Swift's satires imply that people (including satirists) inevitably thrust themselves into the center,
but his satires nonetheless attempt to measure the subsequent
deformations.

----

sharply, and I do not agree with Starkman's view that Swift stands in total
opposition to the new learning: "Swift rejected and reviled the new learning....A Tale of a Tub is the expression of Swift's deep-seated and consistent
conservatism, from which bias he looked at every facet of life and found the
old better than the new" (Starkman, 4). Miriam Starkman's book identifies
many of Swift's targets but sometimes does not discriminate between the
abuse attacked by Swift and the intellectual area of which the abuse is only a
part. Brian Vickers, "Swift and the Baconian Idol," in *The World of Jonathan
Swift*, ed. Brian Vickers (Oxford: Basil Blackwell, 1968), 87–128, finds many
parallels, primarily stylistic ones, between Bacon's writings and Swift's *Tale
of a Tub*. Because Vickers adopts a view of Swift's conservatism that is similar
to Miriam Starkman's, he concludes that Swift's parodies "were subversive
attacks on the idol of the seventeenth century" (p. 114). While the parody of
Bacon that Vickers uncovers is often telling evidence that Swift disapproved
of aspects of Bacon's writing, it seems to me that Swift's limited attack on Bacon, or on Baconians, is balanced by an attitude toward human experience
that Swift shared with Bacon. Donald Greene, *The Age of Exuberance* (New
York: Random House, 1970), 101–10, surveys the widespread influence of Bacon and the prevalence of empiricism not only as a scientific methodology but
also as a habit of mind in the eighteenth century.

Swift's attacks on aspects of the Royal Society do not preclude his sharing with it a version of Baconian empiricism. Swift is in sympathy with Bacon's more generalized comments on the dangers of certain habits of mind, and he is in general accord with the attitudes of major spokesmen for the Royal Society although not with many of the Society's specific practices. As M. B. Hall shows in his study "Science in the Early Royal Society," "individual Fellows might hold what views they liked, and did so—Cartesian, Baconian, Epicurean, mystic, Aristotelian, medical, chemical—the list might be nearly endless. What concerned the Society as an organised body was to avoid *its* commitment to *a priori* systems, those based upon empirically untestable tenets or principles."[3] The Royal Society had, of course, to attend to the theories and hypotheses that naive versions of Baconianism sometimes appeared to eschew. But as P. M. Rattansi suggests in his study "Science and Religion in the Seventeenth Century," there is a "mythical element in the self-image of scientific movements or institutions" that does not include the complexities and divergences of their actual thought and practice.[4]

In the *Battle*, Gresham, home of the Royal Society, is described as one of the "Seminaries" of the malignant deity Criticism (*Tale*, p. 242). Nevertheless, Bacon himself is not vanquished by the ancients: "Then *Aristotle* observing *Bacon* advance with a furious Mien, drew his Bow to the Head, and let fly his Arrow, which miss'd the valiant *Modern*, and went hizzing over his Head; but *Des-Cartes* it hit" (*Tale*, p. 244). Although Temple had praised Bacon in "An Essay upon the Ancient and Modern Learning," and also had contempt for Descartes, Swift's linking of the two does not derive from Temple's essay. The passage in which Temple praises Bacon occurs in a survey of stylistic achievements in various languages: Sidney, Bacon, and Selden are chosen to represent English.[5]

[3]M. B. Hall, "Science in the Early Royal Society," in *The Emergence of Science in Western Europe*, ed. Maurice Crosland (London: Macmillan, 1975), 62.
[4]P. M. Rattansi, "Science and Religion in the Seventeenth Century," in *The Emergence of Science in Western Europe,* ed. Crosland, 84.
[5]*Five Miscellaneous Essays by Sir William Temple*, ed. Samuel Holt Monk (Ann

Swift's contrast of Bacon and Descartes implies an assessment of their differing epistemologies, while the passage in Temple makes no reference even to Bacon's enormous influence as a propagandizer for the new science.

The judgments that Swift implies by associating Aristotle, Bacon, and Descartes in this encounter are conventional ones. Both Thomas Sprat in *The History of the Royal Society* (1667) and William Wotton in *Reflections Upon the Ancient and Modern Learning* (1694), for example, praise Bacon for his concern with observation and experiment and condemn Descartes for his obsession with his own thought processes.[6] Although the Aristotelians were often attacked as obstacles to the advancement of science, Aristotle himself was sometimes commended as an unusually good naturalist for his day. Wotton remarks on Aristotle's deficiencies, but he also mitigates these criticisms: Aristotle "had examined very many things himself," but "it was too Vast a Work for any single Man to go through with by himself" (Wotton, p. 272). Swift's image, then, of an Aristotle who destroys Descartes but is unable to harm Bacon implies an assessment of these men similar to that made by Royal Society members and followers. The fable of the spider and the bee too implies an evaluation of epistemologies similar to that to be found in the episode in which Aristotle attacks Bacon but hits Descartes. The essential characteristic of the spider is that he is as little dependent as possible on anything external to self; he is a Cartesian who "Spins and Spits wholly from himself" (*Tale*, p. 234). The essential characteristic of the bee is the use of the external, "an universal Range, with long Search, much Study" (*Tale*, p. 232).

Arbor: University of Michigan Press, 1963), 65. All subsequent references to Temple are to this same edition, which contains the following works: "Upon the Gardens of Epicurus"; "An Essay upon the Ancient and Modern Learning"; "Some Thoughts upon Reviewing the Essay of Ancient and Modern Learning"; "Of Heroic Virtue"; "Of Poetry."

[6]Thomas Sprat, *History of the Royal Society*, ed. Jackson I. Cope and Harold Whitmore Jones, Washington University Studies (St. Louis: Washington University, 1958), 35, 95–96. All references are to this edition. William Wotton, *Reflections Upon the Ancient and Modern Learning*, facs. ed. (Hildesheim: Georg Olms, 1968), 306. All references are to this edition.

Two of the most immediate of the many sources or analogues of these commonplace images are to be found in Temple and Bacon.[7] Temple uses the bee to comment on the writing of poetry, and Bacon uses the ant, spider, and bee to comment on procedures in natural philosophy. In Swift's fable we can see the full force of the combination of Temple and Bacon: the bee's flight is both in time and in space. Sweetness and light come from Homer and also from Bacon's search into nature, "ranging thro' every Corner of Nature" (*Tale*, p. 234). Swift's fable is a commentary on ways of understanding the external world, not just on literature or on natural science. In fact, the ancient and modern authors who are being measured by the fable encompass all areas of learning. Swift's point is not markedly different from that made by Sprat in his *History* when he discusses the limitations of Descartes's method: "It is impossible, but they, who will onely transcribe their own thoughts, and disdain to measure or strengthen them by the assistance of others, should be in most of their apprehensions too narrow, and obscure; by setting down things for general, which are onely peculiar to themselves" (Sprat, p. 96). Sprat recommends reading as well as experimenting, rejecting the notion that reading produces prejudices that are inimical to objectivity: "That man, who is thoroughly acquainted with all sorts of *Opinions*, is very much more unlikely, to adhere obstinately to any one particular" (Sprat, p. 97).

Before his encounter with Aristotle in the *Battle*, Descartes appears in association with Gassendi and Hobbes, "whose Strength was such, that they could shoot their Arrows beyond the *Atmosphere*, never to fall down again" (*Tale*, pp. 235–36). The image of shooting arrows beyond the atmosphere is appropriate to the conventional evaluation of Descartes as a rationalist whose mind observes no earthly limits, but it may seem less appropriate with respect to Gassendi and Hobbes, who are in some respects opposite to Descartes. Both opposed the prominence of mind and its sharp separation from the body that are characteristic of Cartesian dualism. In response to Descartes's

---

[7]Temple, *Five Miscellaneous Essays*, 182; Bacon, *Philosophical Works*, 288.

notion that we can perceive things by the mind without sense
or imagination, Hobbes advanced the hypothesis that all operations of the mind are unavoidably physical: "Reasoning will
depend on names, names on the imagination, and imagination, perchance, as I think, on the motion of the corporeal or-
gans. Thus mind will be nothing but the motions in certain
parts of an organic body."[8] Gassendi too was unconvinced by
Descartes's separation of thought from body: "...you still
have to prove that the power of thinking is so much superior to
the nature of body, that neither breath nor any other mobile,
pure, and rarified body, can by any means be so adapted as to
be capable of exercising thought."[9]

There is, however, a point of comparison among these markedly different thinkers. In Cartesian dualism, as well as in
Hobbesian materialism and Gassendi's neo-Epicureanism,
nature is separated from a spiritual principle: Descartes's cosmology is in many respects as mechanistic as Epicurus's. According to Descartes, the matter of the universe is organized by
the force of vortices, a theory that was often ridiculed by his opponents. When in the *Battle* Descartes is vanquished by Aristotle, "Death, like a Star of superior Influence, drew him into his
own *Vortex*" (*Tale*, p. 244). This image and the contrast of Descartes to Bacon elsewhere suggest that Swift was attacking Descartes both for his cosmology and for the kind of rationalism
that Bacon attacked; Swift's point is that the rationalism leads
to the cosmology. As I noted earlier, Descartes's epistemology,
at least in general terms, was well known in the form of an invidious contrast to Baconian empiricism.

As Swift's epistemological myth accretes examples of error
that are more and more distant from each other, it becomes increasingly apparent that his central concern is a habit of mind
that we may loosely call rationalism.[10] In Swift's view both ma-

[8]"Objections and Replies," in *The Philosophical Works of Descartes*, trans.
Elizabeth S. Haldane and G. R. T. Ross (Cambridge: Cambridge University
Press, 1912), 2:65.
[9]"Objections and Replies," in *The Philosophical Works of Descartes*, trans.
Haldane and Ross, 2:140.
[10]Frederik N. Smith, *Language and Reality in Swift's "A Tale of a Tub"* (Columbus: Ohio State University Press, 1979), finds that "*A Tale of a Tub* turns in

terialists who reduce mind to matter and Cartesians who exalt it above matter act according to theories that are created for some ulterior purpose. In the "Digression on Madness," Descartes the rationalist and Epicurus the materialist are associated as madmen who wish to subdue all other thought to their own systems (*Tale*, p. 167). They are among those who ignore their "private Infirmities" and the "stubborn Ignorance of the People" in order to advocate their "particular Notions," refusing to shape their understanding "by the Pattern of Human Learning" (*Tale*, p. 171).

The Mechanical Operation of the Spirit extends this analysis to religious enthusiasm, pitting Hobbism against the dissenters' excesses, but showing a common ground. The satire is directed both at the enthusiasts and at the Hobbist narrator.[11] The theoretical oppositions of Hobbism and enthusiasm are resolved into a practical similarity, as the theories of Descartes, Hobbes, and Gassendi were treated in the *Battle*. Although Hobbes and the dissenters use different language, both are dominated by the body.

The *Mechanical Operation* does not allude to Descartes, but the enthusiasts occupy a position in this work analogous to that of Descartes in the *Battle*. The enthusiasts are only one version of a generalized error that occurs in the "Kingdom of Knowledge" (*Tale*, p. 266); the final image of enthusiasm is that of the

---

general on the opposition between the Cartesian rationalism of the Modern and the Lockean empiricism of Swift himself" (p. 126). He sees this opposition embodied in stylistic contrasts within the *Tale*.

[11] Edwin Honig, "Notes on Satire in Swift and Jonson," *New Mexico Quarterly* 18 (1948), remarks, "In satirizing the extreme forms of Puritan irrationality, Swift assumes the role of a virtuoso for whom everything is scientifically determined" (p. 158). James L. Calderwood, "Structural Parody in Swift's 'Fragment,'" *Modern Language Quarterly* 23 (1962), finds that "the blade of direct satire aims outward at religious enthusiasm, the pointed handles of parody aim inward at the author" (p. 246). Robert H. Hopkins, "The Personation of Hobbism in Swift's *Tale of a Tub* and *Mechanical Operation of the Spirit*," *Philological Quarterly* 45 (1966), 372–76, finds the satire on Aeolism in the *Tale* and on enthusiasm in the *Mechanical Operation of the Spirit* derived from Hobbes's interpretation of spirit as wind. He finds that both narrators "are Hobbists who in attacking enthusiasm are also revealing the materialism of Hobbes" (p. 376).

"Philosopher, who, while his Thoughts and Eyes were fixed upon the *Constellations*, found himself seduced by his *lower Parts* into a *Ditch*" (*Tale*, p. 289). In Swift's mythology, the severing of spirit from body, whatever its aim, results in a foul body. Rationalism is for Swift not a cold and rigidly logical exercise of reason but the defeat of reason because of its divorce from sense experience.

In the *Mechanical Operation* Swift's narrator adopts the Hobbist view that all is body and that all thought derives from sense.[12] He then interprets the enthusiasts somewhat as a Hobbist would a Cartesian. Reason is an intellectual power that depends on sense; consequently the way to give the spirit unimpeded sway over reason is "to divert, bind up, stupify, fluster, and amuse the *Senses*" (*Tale*, pp. 269–70). The "spirit" that then takes over for the enthusiasts is, however, a bodily one—lust—thus confirming the narrator's Hobbist view. The enthusiasts become a debased version of the Cartesians' pretended separation of the rational and spiritual elements of man from the physical.

This association of Descartes with feverish excesses is not unprecedented.[13] It occurs, for example, in Gabriel Daniel's popular satire, translated into English in 1692 as *A Voyage to the World of Cartesius* (London, Thomas Bennet). Daniel's central satiric device is a literalization of the Cartesian separation of body and soul: the body is treated as a mechanism that can function after a fashion while the soul goes exploring. Descartes achieves this separation, however, not by any spiritual or scientific exercise, but in an ecstatic fit induced by taking snuff (p. 19), rather like the "Knot of Irish" in the *Mechanical Operation*, who "abstract themselves from Matter, bind up all their Senses, grow visionary and spiritual, by Influence of a short Pipe of Tobacco" (*Tale*, p. 272).

[12]Hobbes, *Leviathan*, ed. C. B. MacPherson (Baltimore: Penguin Books, 1968), IV, 46, p. 689.
[13]Michael R. G. Spiller, "The Idol of the Stove: The Background to Swift's Criticism of Descartes," *Review of English Studies* 25 (1974), 15–24, argues that Swift associated Descartes with religious fanaticism in *A Tale of a Tub* and that this association may have been common in Swift's time.

The method of analysis used by the narrator of the *Mechanical Operation* is the redefinition of terms, a method characteristic of Hobbes. Although Hobbes believes that all thinking originates in sense, he knows that there are many kinds of words, some of them only names of our imaginations and others names of names (*Leviathan*, IV, 46, p. 690). Consequently we have a terminology for many things that do not exist, although the terminology ultimately has its origins in sense. According to this view, enthusiasts have devised a vocabulary that disguises their conceptions' origins in sense, and the narrator of the *Mechanical Operation* is restoring these conceptions to their true meanings. The "spirit" of the enthusiasts is not "a supernatural Assistance, approaching from without," but something "proceeding entirely from within" (*Tale*, p. 271). The "Inward Light" is "a large Memory, plentifully fraught with Theological Polysyllables, and mysterious Texts from holy Writ" (*Tale*, p. 278).

Swift shows the process by which the narrator's method extends itself until it becomes a theory about all spirit, not just about enthusiasts. At first, the narrator specifically limits himself to the "Mechanic Operation" of the spirit (*Tale*, p. 267). He remarks later, however, that "it is in *Life* as in *Tragedy*, where, it is held, a Conviction of great Defect, both in Order and Invention, to interpose the Assistance of preternatural Power without an absolute and last Necessity" (*Tale*, p. 275). Having found his own explanation, one that requires no power beyond the human, he thinks that the argument about whether the "*English* Enthusiastick Preachers" suffer from "*Possession, or Inspiration*" is pointless (*Tale*, p. 275). He describes scathingly the dissenters' practice of ascribing all events, however trivial, to God or the devil and concludes: "Who, that sees a little paultry Mortal, droning, and dreaming, and drivelling to a Multitude, can think it agreeable to common good Sense, that either Heaven or Hell should be put to the Trouble of Influence or Inspection upon what he is about" (*Tale*, p. 276). This remark is an indictment not only of the enthusiasts but also of any conception of providence.

Thomas Burnet appears to be covertly parodied in this treatment of providence. The elimination of providence by the narrator of the *Mechanical Operation* is an extension (a somewhat unfair one) of ideas in Burnet's *Sacred Theory of the Earth*, one of the works that evoked Temple's *Essay upon the Ancient and Modern Learning*. Burnet was a Cartesian who at one point in his book urges an introspective search into self to validate the existence of self and God: "When a man hath withdrawn himself from the noise of this busy World, lock'd up his Senses and his Passions, and everything that should unite him with it: commanded a general silence in the Soul, and suffers not a thought to stir, but what looks inward; Let him then reflect seriously."[14] Burnet's central purpose is to explicate the flood and the conflagration to come in the end times in terms that will accord with modern natural philosophy. He frequently warns the reader not to evade the study of natural causes by ascribing everything to God's direct action: "Therefore as the first Rule concerning miracles is this, That we must not flie to miracles, where Man and Nature are sufficient; so the second Rule is this, that we must not flie to a sovereign infinite power, where an Angelical is sufficient. And the reason in both rules is the same, namely, because it argues a defect of Wisdom in all Oeconomies to employ more and greater means than are sufficient" (p. 281; see also pp. 34, 125–26, 280). As Ernest Tuveson notes, one of Burnet's most frequent metaphors is the comparison of the world to a theater;[15] for example: "And this being the last Act and close of all humane affairs, it ought to be the more exquisite and elaborate: that it may crown the work, satisfie the Spectators, and end in a general applause. The whole Theatre resounding with the praises of the great Dramatist, and the wonderful art and order of the composition" (Burnet, p. 371; see also pp. 133, 140, 189, 241, 249, 250, 275, 282, 298, 356, 358). When this theatrical metaphor is combined with Burnet's repeated warnings against depending exclusively on first causes, it produces a judgment of the narrator of the *Mechanical Opera-*

---

[14]Thomas Burnet, *Sacred Theory of the Earth* (Carbondale: Southern Illinois University Press, 1965), 214. All references are to this edition, which is a reprint of Burnet's second edition.

[15]Ernest Tuveson, *Millennium and Utopia: A Study in the Background of the Idea of Progress*, rev. ed. (New York: Harper and Row, 1964), 124–25.

tion that "it is in *Life* as in *Tragedy*...[a] great Defect...to interpose the Assistance of preternatural Power without an absolute and last Necessity" (*Tale*, p. 275).

Swift's assimilation of Burnet to a Hobbesian perspective is inaccurate and unfair to Hobbes and Burnet, but it reflects Swift's vision of the consequences of any method that makes providence and Scripture dependent on a human interpretation of nature. Burnet, like other physico-theologians, interpreted the Bible by the standards of natural philosophy, and, in consequence, believed that as our understanding of nature increased so did our understanding of Scripture (Burnet, pp. 203–204). Given the system of consequences shown in the *Mechanical Operation*, nature will eventually appear sufficient in itself, because only what is in accord with the method of observation will be remarked. In this view, any theory that allows either nature or spirit to dominate will reduce everything to the favored dimension and will be unable to account for humanity as a union of body and spirit.

Swift's method of constructing his epistemological myth often exposes several figures in a single passage, one obvious attack suggesting an additional form of error. In the *Mechanical Operation* when Hobbism is the perspective used to define enthusiasm, for example, this double attack eventually includes Burnet and Cartesianism as well. Swift's seeming resolution of diverse errors into one almost indistinguishable heap indicates two of his assumptions about error: (1) the central error of thought is rationalism, if defined as a divorce of reason from experience; (2) rationalism is an error not of reason but of will, because it is a use of the mind to create pleasing fictions. The most encompassing figure in Swift's myth is Epicurus, as reflected in Lucretius, the dubious figure of the poet, to whom the title page of the *Tale* and frequent quotations thereafter allude. Lucretius represents the tendency of philosophy, natural and moral, to become merely pleasing fictions.

Here and elsewhere, Swift employs one of the common seventeenth-century conflations—Epicurus (or Lucretius) and Hobbes, who were associated with each other on the basis of their materialism. As Phillip Harth argues, "Swift's description of the beliefs of the tailor-worshippers'' ridicules Hobbesian materialism: "The Worshippers of this Deity had also a System of their Belief, which seemed to turn upon the following Fundamental. They held the Universe to be a large *Suit of Cloaths*, which *invests* every Thing: That the Earth is *invested* by the Air; the Air is *invested* by the Stars; and the Stars are *invested* by the *Primum Mobile*" (*Tale*, pp. 77–78).[16] In addition, this attack on Hobbes contains an echo of Lucretius: "Again, do but behold that which around and above comprehends all the earth in its embrace [sky]: if it makes from itself all things, as some declare, and takes them back when they are destroyed, then the whole consists of a body subject to birth and death."[17]

Epicurean materialism had already been identified in Wotton's *Reflections* as a form of rationalism opposed to Royal Society empiricism. Epicurus, as described by Wotton, resembles Swift's spider: he "despised all Manner of Learning...and gloried in this, that he spun all his thoughts out of his own Brain; a good Argument of his Wit indeed, but a very ordinary one of that skill in Nature, which Lucretius extolls in him every time that he takes occasion to speak of him" (Wotton, p. 302). Lucretius is not himself unaware of the rationalism that Wotton spies: "The mind seeks to understand what is there in the distance whither the intelligence desires to look forth, and whither the mind's projection flies free of itself" (Lucretius, II, ll. 1044–47).

In the seventeenth century, Epicurus's thought was customarily divided into two segments—the cosmological and the ethical—a division that is already established in *De finibus*

---

[16]Phillip Harth, *Swift and Anglican Rationalism: The Religious Background of "A Tale of a Tub"* (Chicago: University of Chicago Press, 1961), 83–85.

[17]Lucretius, *De rerum natura*, trans. W. H. D. Rouse, 3d ed., Loeb Classical Library (Cambridge: Harvard University Press, 1937), V, ll. 318–21. Subsequent references are to this edition and translation. In *A Tale of a Tub*, Swift sometimes quotes the Latin and sometimes the translation by Creech. I do not use Creech's translation because he sometimes omits or deemphasizes Lucretius's dismay at the degeneration of his universe, an aspect of Lucretius that links him to Burnet and figures in Wotton's attack on those who hold theories of decline. Maresca, *Epic to Novel*, 151–53, argues that Lucretius and Hobbes are also conflated in the Aeolist section of the *Tale*.

bonorum et malorum, Cicero's exposition of Epicurean, Stoic, and Academic ethical systems. Erasmus, More, Brown, Temple, and many others respected at least some aspects of Epicurean ethics, although not the Epicurean theories about the physical universe. Swift, however, finds that the ethical and physical systems gain support from each other.

As defined by Lucretius, Epicurus's achievement is the banishing of man's terrors by giving him knowledge. The universe, considering how "great are the faults it stands endowed with" (Lucretius, II, l. 181), could not have been created or ordered by divine power; it has been formed by atoms that "by trying every kind of motion and combination . . . fall into such arrangements as this sum of things consists of" (Lucretius, I, ll. 1026–28). Man need not fear hell because his self is concluded at death (Lucretius, I, ll. 227–29); and the gods are "neither propitiated with services nor touched by wrath" (Lucretius, II, ll. 650–51). An understanding of Epicurean cosmology and physics will bring man to a state in which he can endure the very real horrors of his world in tranquillity. As Swift knew, the ethics and physics are adjunct to each other. If all is material, no active demands are made on man. He can do little to change his condition, although he can diminish at least his mental pain by reducing his fears of the gods.

The narrator of Swift's *Tale* adopts an Epicurean view of his physical world—he reduces all to material and eliminates divine purpose—but in Swift this view does not axiomatically lead to happiness; instead it leads to a sense of the world's meaninglessness. Happiness can then only be achieved by the "mighty Advantages Fiction has over Truth" (*Tale*, p. 172). In Swift's work, the Epicurean truths do not merely alleviate man's terrors but also constrict him. Another set of fictions must then be used to free man, allowing him to soar "out of his own Reach and Sight" (*Tale*, p. 157). The pseudo-order of Epicurean scientific theory leads not to happiness but to madness.

Man's feelings, his desires for happiness, are at the center of Lucretius's exposition; consequently Swift travesties Lucretius by showing the *Tale*'s narrator attempting to make everything subservient to self. The physical theories of the *Tale* are not givens to which the narrator must adapt himself but creations of the mind that may be abandoned for other fictions. Because the goal is happiness, no fact is allowed to interfere. In explaining the materiality of the physical world, Lucretius relies heavily on sense perceptions. Things are, he argues, what they seem. The images of things are in fact "semblances and thin shapes of things...thrown off from their outer surface... which are to be called as it were their films or bark" (Lucretius, IV, ll. 42ff.). Swift's narrator, unlike Lucretius, uses this theory not to explain something but to avoid considering "the Flaws and Imperfections of Nature" (*Tale*, p. 174). If he can be content with "the *Films* and *Images* that fly off upon his Senses from the *Superficies* of Things" (*Tale*, p. 174), he need not look beneath the surface.[18] Lucretius's theory of perception becomes in Swift a willed device for avoiding an unpleasant truth that interferes with the human desire to be happy.

Swift's version of Epicureanism contrasts with that in Erasmus's *Praise of Folly*. The *Praise of Folly* articulates two versions of the Epicurean search for pleasure—the vulgar version that seeks illusion and sensuality and the Christian version that finds true pleasures apart from earthly ones. Folly is a vulgar Epicurean who fails to discriminate between Christian folly and her kind of folly. When she praises Christian happiness, Folly exposes her own equivocations, which are based on contradictory versions of Epicureanism. Erasmus does not, however, deal with Epicurean cosmology.

Swift defines a far harsher version of Epicureanism, one not allowing even the possibility of meliorative redefinition. His epistemology allows no flight from the body to spiritual rapture. Nor does he allow even the trivial folly of fleshly pleasure. In Swift, the refuge in body too is part of a vast fictionalizing mechanism that connects Epicurean cosmology and ethics.

---

[18]Charles Scruggs, "Swift's Use of Lucretius in *A Tale of a Tub*," *Texas Studies in Literature and Language* 15 (1973), 39–49, remarks that "the true motive of the hack's epistemology is not the pursuit of real knowledge but the justification of happiness as an ethical goal" (p. 47). Other writers on the subject see Swift as concerned about one or another aspect of Epicureanism but not about the system as a whole.

The "Digression on Madness" shows madness to be the consequence of the Epicurean search for happiness, and further, it shows the meaningless world of Epicurean atomism to be the justification for a far from amiable version of madness.

Swift's linking of the Epicurean cosmology and ethics was not unprecedented. In Richard Bentley's "Boyle Lectures," given in 1692 and printed in 1692–93, they are seen as interdependent.[19] Bentley finds the happiness that is the goal of the Epicurean to be unchristian, and he argues that the rejection of God's providence, characteristic of Epicureanism, is willful, a matter not of intellect but of desire (Bentley, p. 11): if "satisfied by some Epicurean of his time, that all was but *atoms*, and *vacuum*, and *necessity*, and *chance*" a person might be expected to lament that "those glorious hopes of immortality and bliss" were "nothing but cheating joys and pleasant delusions" (Bentley, pp. 9, 10). But atheists prefer extinction to the possibility of bliss because they have "sinned away all expectation of ever arriving at heaven" (Bentley, p. 13). Bentley's view of Epicureans is that even the "*vere adepti*, the masters and rabbies of Atheism" are "despondent wretches": "The boasted happy Atheist in the indolence of body, and an undisturbed calm and serenity of mind, is altogether as rare a creature as the *vir sapiens* was among the Stoics" (Bentley, p. 15). Swift and Bentley see Epicureanism as the defense of guilty people against their fears of a future life. To both men, Epicurean natural philosophy is a fiction willfully embraced in order to bring solace where pain would be more salubrious.

Swift's positions cannot be plotted entirely on the basis of the friendships implied by the ancients-moderns conflict in the *Battle of the Books*.[20] Swift's position on Epicureanism, for example,

[19] *The Works of Richard Bentley*, ed. Alexander Dyce (1838; reprinted, New York: AMS Press, 1966), 3:60–61. Wolfgang Fleischmann, *Lucretius and English Literature, 1680–1740* (Paris: A. G. Nizet, 1964), 167, identifies these lectures as the most powerful and popular attack on Epicureanism ever delivered in England.

[20] Irvin Ehrenpreis, *Swift: The Man, His Works, and the Age* (Cambridge: Harvard University Press, 1962), vol. 1, pt. 2, analyzes many of the stresses in the relationship of Temple and Swift. Philip Pinkus, "Swift and the Ancients-Moderns Controversy," *University of Toronto Quarterly* 29 (1959), 46–58, sug-

differed sharply from Temple's (Temple admired Epicurean ethics), and in some respects Swift is not opposed to the views of Wotton and Bentley. The problem of ascertaining Swift's views is further complicated by the fact that neither Swift nor Temple held the belief in the earth's decline that Wotton attributed to Temple. Swift's views must be disentangled not only from Temple's views but also from Wotton's version of Temple if we are not to fall into the trap of regarding him as opposed to all recent knowledge.

Temple argued that the accumulation of knowledge does not make moderns superior to ancients. In his view, the ancients too had ancients, now lost to the moderns; consequently, the ancients were just as much a culmination of knowledge as the moderns are. Wotton attempts to connect this line of argument to a belief in the "Eternity of the World" ("Preface"), a belief that avoids the need for a special creation. He argues that this irreligious notion is refuted by the facts of human progress. Leaning heavily on Bentley's "Boyle Lectures" (cited and praised in Wotton's "Preface"), Wotton expands Bentley's argument that the moderns' culminative achievements imply a determinate starting point and consequently tend to support creation and to refute atheism. Bentley and Wotton see the eternity of the world as a hypothesis important to atheists be-

---

gests plausibly that Swift was impatient with both sides in the ancients-moderns controversy. Richard Foster Jones, *Ancients and Moderns: A Study of the Rise of the Scientific Movement in Seventeenth-Century England*, 2d ed. (St. Louis: Washington University Press, 1961), is the standard treatment of the subject; however, this study does not do justice to the complexity of the position of Swift and others (in a period somewhat later than that which Jones emphasizes). Jones assumes that an admiration of ancient literature is associated with a rejection of modern science, a correlation that is not inevitably sound (pp. 268–72). A number of studies have suggested that Swift's attacks on aspects of the new science were not rejections of all science. See, e.g., Reuben Potter, "Swift and Natural Science," *Philological Quarterly* 20 (1941), 97–118, and Colin Kiernan, "Swift and Science," *Historical Journal* 14 (1971), 709–22. Donald Greene, "Swift: Some Caveats," *Studies in the Eighteenth Century*, vol. 2, ed. R. F. Brissendon (Toronto: University of Toronto Press, 1973), 341–58, argues persuasively against "the prevalent image of Swift as the archetypal right-winger—the reactionary Tory, the extreme High Churchman, the hater of modern science and empiricism in general" (p. 341).

cause it allows atheists to sidestep the discredited view of the Epicureans that the universe was formed by a fortuitous collocation of atoms. Atheists can then be Epicureans who deny providence without holding the often-ridiculed beliefs of Epicurean physics.

The view that the world has a determinate beginning can also, however, be reconciled to a conception contrary to Wotton's belief in progress: the world may be seen as necessarily and inevitably declining since its beginning about six thousand years ago. Wotton agrees that this view may be accommodated to "the account given by Moses," but he argues that its implications too are atheistical. The hypothesis of the world's decline assumes that the world is an animate being "now worn out, and spent; and so might tempt a Libertine to think that Men, like Mushrooms, sprung out of the Earth when it was fresh and vigorous, impregnated with proper Seminal Atoms, now, of many Ages, no longer seen" (Wotton, "Preface"). Wotton's argument for the idea of progress is then a confutation of two atheistical theories: the earth conceived of as eternal and the earth conceived of as a dying mother independent of any higher authority.

Having already tried to link Temple to an atheistical belief in the eternity of the world, Wotton tries in the body of his book to associate Temple's judgments on the arts with the not entirely compatible theory of the decay of the earth. Discussing sculpture, Wotton remarks, it "may very probably be inferred, That *in these Things also* the World does not decay so fast as Sir *William Temple* believes" (Wotton, p. 77; see also p. 96). This attribution of a belief in the earth's decay to Temple is a misrepresentation. Temple argues that nature differs from one age to another: there may be giants in one age and dwarfs in another (Temple, pp. 51–52). His judgment is that, in general, modern achievements are *in fact* lesser than ancient ones, not that they are necessarily lesser. In Temple's view, if Pico della Mirandola, although a modern, had lived longer, he would have been among the greatest of learned men (Temple, p. 96). What Wotton calls the libertine theory of the earth's decline is the one presented in Lucretius but not in Temple:

Even now indeed the power of life is broken, and the earth exhausted scarce produces tiny creatures, she who once produced
all kinds and gave birth to huge bodies of wild beasts. For it is
not true, as I think, that the races of mortal creatures were let
down from high heaven by some golden chain upon the fields,
nor were they sprung from sea or waves beating upon the rocks,
but the same earth generated them which feeds them now from
herself. [Lucretius, II, ll. 1152–56]

Wotton's misrepresentation of Temple is made egregious by
the fact that one of the books Temple was confuting, Burnet's
Sacred Theory of the Earth, prominently mentions the doctrines of
Epicurus in an attempt to reconcile a theory of decline to one of
progress. Burnet includes many references to the decline of the
earth, for example, people become smaller as their "private
constitution" wears off (Burnet, p. 144). He describes the decline of the earth through successive deformations and disasters, but he believes that man's increasing knowledge will lead
to a better understanding of God's plan, a plan that will culmi-
nate in a new-formed earth.

In the fable of the spider and the bee, Swift constructs one of
his characteristic conflations of error that finally reveals Lucretius in a group including Burnet and Cartesian rationalists.
The spider is a Cartesian who spins all from self and, like the
Cartesian Burnet, has a powerful imagination of cataclysms:
when the web is shaken by the bee, the spider "supposed at
first, that *Nature* was approaching her final Dissolution" (*Tale*,
p. 229). Behind Descartes and Burnet also then appears Lucretius, who depicts an aging world that approaches its final cata-
clysm through a series of physical disasters, ending in the
dissolution of the entire universe: "So therefore the walls of the
mighty world in like manner shall be stormed all around, and
shall collapse into crumbling ruin" (Lucretius, II, ll. 1144-46).

Swift scathingly attacks the idea of progress, but he also rejects theories of the earth's decline. James William Johnson
points out that theories of decline are mocked in the *Tale* by the
account of the degeneration of modern ears and in the *Travels*
by the account of a Brobdingnagian book that laments the gi-

ants' decreases in size.[21] In Johnson's view, Swift's belief in "original sin and his equally strong belief in free will meant that Swift could not adhere to the idea that each age was progressively worse than the one before it, nor could he assume that each age was better" (p. 62). Swift's empiricism lacks the optimism to be found in Wotton or in Bacon, but it also rejects the subversion of the human agent to be found in theories of decline.

The epistemology represented in Swift's satires is negative: Swift explores the limitations of the human understanding that are imposed by the unalterable condition of being body and soul-spirit-mind. But the nature of the connection is inexplicable, as Swift remarks in one of his sermons: "The Manner whereby the Soul and Body are united, and how they are distinguished, is wholly unaccountable to us" (9:164). As Phillip Harth shows, Swift is not a fideist or, in the narrow sense, a skeptic.[22] The satires do, however, sometimes appear to be skeptical, because the very different perspectives of Hobbes, Descartes, Burnet, physico-theology, and even religious enthusiasm are allowed to shade into each other as examples of similar errors. Robert Martin Adams concludes that "while Locke was rendering Christianity reasonable in terms of a mechanical philosophy and while Berkeley was quietly gathering the spiritual principle into a defiant solipsism, Swift, instead of trying to reconcile the alternatives of spirit and matter or to choose

[21]James William Johnson, "Swift's Historical Outlook," *Journal of British Studies* 4 (1965), 62–63.

[22] Harth, *Swift and Anglican Rationalism*, esp. 20–21, 32–34. Swift believed that natural religion is discoverable by reason, although the revelation of Scripture is needed to teach men additional Christian truths that are inaccessible to reason. I do not, however, accept Phillip Harth's view that "Swift's epistemological premises in *A Tale of a Tub* . . . are Cartesian," even "at second hand" (*Swift and Anglican Rationalism*, 151). It appears to me that Harth arrives at his judgment on Swift's epistemology because he focuses only on portions of the *Tale* and on those parallel discussions to be found among the clergy he calls Anglican rationalists. He uses skepticism or fideism as contrasts to rationalism. Seeing rationalism in contrast to empiricism seems somewhat more appropriate to the issues in Swift's *Tale*. The context for the term then includes the conventional contrasts of the Cartesian and Baconian epistemologies, neither of which is skeptical. Of course, rationalism and empiricism were not so sharply opposed in fact as many eighteenth-century thinkers pretended.

between them, made it his concern to repudiate both.''[23] But
Swift repudiates the *separation* of body and spirit, however in-
comprehensible their connection is. Matter and spirit are necessary counterbalances to each other. They limit the sphere of
the human understanding, but their uneasy relationship also
increases human awareness of the limitation.

In his satiric works, Swift is unconcerned to weigh the differences between Hobbes and Descartes, materialist and rationalist. Rather he seeks to assert their equivalence, which results
from a theoretical and arbitrary severance of what is inexplicably united. Swift's assimilation of these markedly different figures to each other finally seems inspired, not casual.
Millenarians and Cartesians like Burnet, as well as Hobbesian
materialists, are conflated in Epicureanism, as represented in
the figure of Lucretius, the grandly ambitious poet who according to tradition went mad and was followed into the same state
by his seventeenth-century translator Creech. Against these
figures stand Bacon and Aristotle, neither of them grand, nor
warmly endorsed, but nevertheless validated by their very limitations. The diverse accretions of this epistemological myth do
not blunt its meaning but clarify the purpose of its method.

As we will see in the *Travels*, human limitations are not, despite Swift's respect for Bacon, overcome by an empiricist program. Gulliver, unlike the tale-teller, exemplifies the
cautiousness in style and observation that is enjoined by the
Royal Society.[24] Nevertheless, like the tale-teller, he is able to

[23]Robert Martin Adams, *Strains of Discord: Studies in Literary Openness*
(Ithaca: Cornell University Press, 1958), 156.
[24]Francis D. Louis, *Swift's Anatomy of Misunderstanding: A Study of Swift's
Epistemological Imagination in "A Tale of a Tub" and "Guilliver's Travels"* (Tow-
towa: Barnes and Noble, 1981), studies the similar epistemological concerns of
both books: "The 'new' scientific learning simply makes its misjudgments in
the name of fact rather than fancy, and although Gulliver errs in the sacred
name of truth and in the best empirical manner of the Royal Society, he errs
all the same: and therein lies Swift's epistemological *Tale* as well as his *Travels*" (p. 11). Francis Louis sees the narrators as inconsistent but argues that
Swift may break the rules as he likes: "It is his circus....We are being asked
to watch the puppet closely, not asked to believe that the puppet is the creator" (p. 48). My views differ in that I find the puppet to be enacting a creator, and such an enactment seems to me central to Swift's epistemological
and literary concerns.

109

convert to his own purposes the verbal and intellectual forms that he uses. Swift shares empiricism's suspicion of human subjectivity, but he has little confidence that this limitation can be overcome.

Travels into Several Remote
Nations of the World

CHAPTER 5

Subduing a Literary Form

A Tale of a Tub appeared in 1704, the *Travels* in 1726. In his life of Swift, Samuel Johnson observes that "what is true of [the *Tale*] is not true of anything else which he had written." While the *Tale* "exhibits a vehemence and rapidity of mind, a copiousness of images, and vivacity of diction," in Swift's other works "is found an equable tenor of easy language."[1] But in addition to these obvious contrasts, the *Tale* and the *Travels* also manifest common concerns. Both works present a version (a differing one) of the "author" whose shaping of literary conventions obliquely reveals a self. And both works imply similar epistemological concerns, although the *Travels* starts where the *Tale* leaves off, examining the empiricism that the *Tale* recommends, and discovering that it, like rationalism, can be used to conceal rather than to reveal.

Swift's name did not appear on the work that we now know as *Gulliver's Travels* (his title was *Travels into Several Remote Nations of the World*). The volume introduces itself to us as if it were an authentic work of travel literature and then makes use of the fiction of the travel book to facilitate its satiric attack. Its satiric images and scenes are placed outside familiar lands, thus rationalizing their lack of verisimilitude. This distance also encourages the development of a new perspective by traveler and

[1]Samuel Johnson, *Lives of the English Poets,* Everyman's Library (London: J. M. Dent, 1925), 2:267.

reader. Neither is blinded by habitude, and the newly perceived scene rejuvenates the eye that then regards old familiar scenes. An educational theme is implicit in this form: the satire insinuates its perspective only gradually. The travel book stands in contrast, for example, to the mock epic, which exploits what is already known but not yet expressed: in the mock epic the clash of form and content is an immediate assertion of an already accepted evaluation. Although the two forms—the satiric travel book and the mock epic—are not discrete (for example, the satiric travel book may contain mock epic elements), the tendency of one is to develop temporally (that is, through narrative) a vision that the other asserts immediately.

Using one genre to organize another creates a dissonance, which, in the case of mock epic, is the very source of the satire. The clash of form and content is resolved by using one element to measure the other. But the extended narrative development of the travel book is not so easily resolved into a clash of elements that function as satire. The effect is often of one genre melding with another, sometimes kaleidoscopically, rather than clashing functionally and decisively. Travel book, imaginary voyage, utopia, and autobiography are allied with each other, and each may be used as a satiric fiction. Utopian fictions occupy an important position in these permutations of satire. A satiric utopia is a close relative of the imaginary voyage; a true utopia seeks alliance with the travel book. The satiric utopia may be distinguished from the true utopia by determining whether the depicted society can be appropriately imitated or serves primarily as a standard to define another society. But when the traveler is emphasized, the narrative moves toward autobiography.

The key to these potential alliances of the travel book is the narrator. His emphases or suppressions activate the unstable elements on the genre's borders. If the narrator of a travel book is not morally neutral, his book tends to become utopian: either the narrator's own society or the visited society is likely to be regarded as normative. If the narrator visits lands with little or no social organization, his evaluations become a form of the philosophy of nature—either primitivist or Hobbist. The Hobbist view, however, implies the desirability of certain forms of social organization and is thus allied to utopian literature. The primitivist view leads to pastoral literature, but it too is allied to utopianism as soon as it even implies a plan to primitivize civilization.

The utopian permutations of the travel book result from the narrator's interpretation of the scene, but whenever the focus shifts to the traveler-narrator, the travel book will ally itself to autobiography. In its purest form the travel book makes the reader into its traveler, but if the story's authenticity becomes an issue, the narrator must vouch for his experiences. The narrator's authentication of the scene is of less importance if the narrated events are commonplace; nevertheless, the commonplace will not induce imaginative travel unless the narrator is of some interest. In a thematic sense too the travel book has autobiographical tendencies. Going out and returning imply a center not only geographical but also personal. Circumnavigating the world (like walking around the block) is an assertion of personal identity: finding a starting point that is an ending depends on a person's continuance from then to now. Travel is change, but this change is insignificant without personal continuity.[2]

An obvious way to organize the dissonance between travel book and satire is to emphasize the relevance of the visited lands to the reader's homeland. But in addition, the narrator-

---

[2] *Tristes Tropiques* by Claude Lévi-Strauss exemplifies the delicate generic balance that is possible within a single book: it is autobiography, travel book, and utopian narrative. Charles L. Batten, Jr., *Pleasurable Instruction: Form and Convention in Eighteenth-Century Travel Literature* (Berkeley: University of California Press, 1978), defines the conventions of eighteenth-century travel literature, arguing that "until the last decades of the century, travel accounts uniformly aimed at conveying pleasurable instruction, not about the traveler but about the countries he visited" (p. 119). Batten is concerned to delimit the genre, to separate the responses appropriate to modern travel narratives from those appropriate to the narratives that he describes. In dealing with the merging of differing forms in the *Travels,* I have necessarily adopted a less prescriptive view, one that regards genre as, in Fredric Jameson's words, "an instrument of exploration": "The relationship between the genres may itself play a significant and functional role within the individual work itself" ("Magical Narratives: Romance as Genre," *New Literary History* 7 [1975], 152, 154).

traveler, the most unstable element in the travel book, must be accommodated to the satire. He may be substantially suppressed, like the narrator of Lucian's *True Voyage,* or he may respond overtly to the scene. In Swift's *Travels* Gulliver announces himself by describing his early life and education, and then he takes us to a land of little people. His early commentary is neutral, and we see the satiric implications of the rope dancing in Lilliput before Gulliver does. But eventually Gulliver remarks on this "infamous Practice" after he has acquired an "imperfect Idea of Courts and Ministers" because of his experiences (ɪɪ:60, 54). The expectation aroused by this procedure is that Gulliver, as well as the reader, will be educated by an encounter with people both like and unlike those of his homeland. Gulliver, we assume, will be integrated into a satiric version of the travel book by serving as the neutral observer, a figure characteristic of the travel book, who then absorbs the lessons figured by the scene, although at a somewhat slower rate than the reader.

But in subsequent voyages, Swift's method is not adequately defined by this early version of the *Travels.* Gulliver's understanding of evil accelerates until he sees it everywhere. He becomes the satirist, not merely learning from the scene but also bringing evil to our attention. In the fourth voyage, his expressed knowledge of European viciousness brings at least part of the scene into being. Indeed, his authorial role becomes as emphatic as his role as traveler. We see the development of the darkened and enlightened vision of the satirist and also the development of his satiric technique.[3]

Ordinarily we expect vision and technique to coincide, expressive of each other. In the *Travels,* however, the adaptation of the putative author's vision to its expression is inexact, allowing us to see the narrator as an author in the process of constructing his role. Swift writes a book not about a man who

[3]Robert C. Elliott, *The Power of Satire: Magic, Ritual, Art* (Princeton: Princeton University Press, 1960), 184–89, defines the difficulty of finding a literary category for the *Travels.* Elliott discusses the *Travels* in the context of the "satirist-satirized theme," showing that Gulliver is the butt not only of Swift's satire but also sometimes of his own (pp. 188–89).

undergoes certain experiences but about a man who writes a book about experiences that he has undergone. Gulliver is shown imposing literary patterns, appropriate or inappropriate, on his narrative. Just as in the *Tale*, Swift attributes authorial choices to his narrator, making us see the satirist's vision as a series of authorial choices rather than as the unmediated truth that the satire claims as its own. Swift's satirist-narrator is just as much an "author" as is the writer of pastorals (the form so mocked by several of Swift's poems).

The first and second voyages show Gulliver becoming a satirist: he at first naively imagines man to be better than he is depicted in satire. But even as he shows himself developing his satiric perspective in the first voyage, the Gulliver who narrates inserts the grim and detached perspective of the fourth voyage. Of his former unwillingness to be blinded in Lilliput, Gulliver remarks: "If I had then known the Nature of Princes and Ministers, which I have since observed in many other Courts . . . ,I should with great Alacrity and Readiness have submitted to so *easy* a Punishment" (II:73). As a narrator Gulliver is more detached from his younger self than that younger self is from the Lilliputian King's ambitions. Gulliver's younger self fulfills the conventional demands of the satirist's role: to see evil reluctantly and then to condemn it forthrightly in order to eliminate it. But even a salutary recognition of, and resistance to, evil by this earlier version of the satirist is for the narrator a failure to recognize the enormity of human evil. He reduces his former self to an object lesson in a satiric fiction.

The later segment of the third voyage becomes an imitation of satire as Gulliver imagines man to be as he is depicted in satire. Gulliver's dialogues with the dead in this book are compendia of the clichés of satire. There is a sense less of discovery than of the working out of a received satiric pattern. Moderns are invidiously contrasted with ancients: "I desired that the Senate of *Rome* might appear before me in one large Chamber, and a modern Representative, in Counterview, in another. The first seemed to be an Assembly of Heroes and Demy-Gods; the other a Knot of Pedlars, Pick-pockets, Highwaymen and Bullies" (II:195–96). As Gulliver continues with his discoveries of unchastity, treason, and perversion he gives the impression of someone who is reproducing the satire he has been reading.

The Struldbrugg episode of this book is also conventional in theme, its power derived not from its originality but from Gulliver's dramatization of the destruction of his own callow version of human progress. In narrating his encounter with the Struldbruggs, Gulliver displays both his then newly developed detachment from humanity and his subsequently developed detachment from his former self. At the time of the described events, he expected the Struldbruggs to be the external confirmation of a dream he had often had: "I had frequently run over the whole System how I should employ myself, and pass the Time if I were sure to live for ever" (II:209). In explaining these visions of perpetuity, Gulliver remarks rudely to his hosts: "My choise and constant Companions should be a Sett of my own immortal Brotherhood . . . , only mingling a few of the most valuable among you Mortals, whom Length of Time would harden me to lose . . . , just as a Man diverts himself with the annual Succession of Pinks and Tulips in his Garden, without regretting the Loss of those which withered the preceding Year" (II:209–10). This Gulliver has no sense of a bond to his hosts nor to mankind, whose "flesh is as grass, and all the glory of man as the flower of grass." And the Gulliver who narrates reveals no bond to his former self. He describes the humiliating destruction of his dream as if his former self too were only one of a "Succession of Pinks and Tulips" (II:210), remarking the "Sort of Smile, which usually ariseth from Pity," on the faces of his hosts (II:208) and concluding his account with the understatement: "The Reader will easily believe . . . my keen Appetite for Perpetuity of Life was much abated" (II:214).

This detachment does not, however, apply to the narrator's sense of his role as author. His former self is the object of his detached and ironic scrutiny, but the originality and veracity of his conventional story is stoutly if uneasily defended: he does "not remember to have met the like in any Book of Travels"

(II:215). Having impersonalized his relationship to his past, he finds a new identity as author.

The fourth voyage becomes a parody of satire as Gulliver imagines people to be far worse than they are depicted in satire. Gulliver achieves a kind of inventive extravagance in this voyage as he exaggerates the conventional patterns of satiric exaggeration. Gulliver's analysis of lawyers, for example, is an attempt to outdo even his Houyhnhnm master's analysis of human evil. After Gulliver's remarks on lawyers, the Houyhnhnm comments on the waste of their abilities: "It was a Pity, that Creatures endowed with such prodigious Abilities of Mind as these Lawyers, by the Description I gave of them must certainly be, were not rather encouraged to be Instructors of others in Wisdom and Knowledge" (II:250). Gulliver responds to this observation by attributing to lawyers a motiveless malignity and monumental stupidity. His remarks are a comic exhibition of the satirist's fantasy; these lawyers live in the heat of Gulliver's imagination, mythical creatures corrupt in all but their devotion to evil: "And having been byassed all their Lives against Truth and Equity, [they] are under such a fatal Necessity of favouring Fraud, Perjury and Oppression; that I have known some of them to have refused a large Bribe from the Side where Justice lay, rather than injure the *Faculty,* by doing anything unbecoming their Nature or their Office" (II:249).[4]

Although Gulliver's stance changes frequently in the *Travels,* these changes are not commonly arbitrary. As Ronald Paulson observes, the first, second, and fourth "voyages spend much of their time on *cause,* showing with almost Defoe-like relish *how*

[4]Several writers have treated the very important comic side of Swift's works. Vivian Mercier, *The Irish Comic Tradition* (Oxford: Clarendon Press, 1962), discusses Swift's roots in Irish satire, humor, wit, and wordplay and illuminates the nature of his enormous influence on subsequent comic writers of Ireland. Peter Steele, *Jonathan Swift: Preacher and Jester* (Oxford: Clarendon Press, 1978), studies the consequences of Swift's roles as preacher and jester, venturing the observation that perhaps "it would be appropriate to say that when Swift looks and laughs, he often exceeds in vision the announced intentions which the vision serves. The laughter is, as it were, visionary rather than strategic" (p. 8).

and *why* a man becomes an object or a proud slave, a satirist or a misanthrope.''[5] Gulliver's motivations are sometimes stated directly, but they are most often implied by his changing manner of narration and his changed responses to similar situations. In the closely linked opening books, for example, Gulliver's reversed position produces his altered judgments. By the end of the first voyage, Gulliver has learned to distrust ministers and courts and has resisted the Lilliputian king's desire to use him to dominate the Lilliputian world. In contrast, in the second voyage the little Gulliver recommends gunpowder to the giant king as a way to make him "absolute master of the Lives, the Liberties, and the Fortunes of his People" (II:135). This reversed position is given a context that implies a motivation. The description of gunpowder occurs in a chapter that immediately follows the king's comments on Gulliver's race, "the most pernicious Race of little odious Vermin that Nature ever suffered to crawl upon the Surface of the Earth" (II:132). In the chapter that precedes this denunciation (chap. 5), Gulliver depicts himself as suffering a series of degrading misadventures, including his being used as a sexual toy by the maids of honor. Consequently, in chapter 6 he praises England extravagantly; he needs something of worth to which to attach himself. And when that praise acquires only the king's condemnation, Gulliver volunteers the secret of gunpowder. Although Gulliver's endorsement of this secret is confirmation of the moral and psychological dimensions of the King's view that Gulliver is an "impotent and groveling Insect" (II:134), Gulliver is not unmotivatedly offering himself as an example of satiric monstrosity. His behavior results from a comprehensible desire to demonstrate a capability that none of these giants had suspected.

When the subject of the devastation caused by European weapons is continued in the fourth voyage, Gulliver places himself in a new relationship to his description. After listing for his Houyhnhnm master various instruments, terms, and con-

[5]Ronald Paulson, *The Fictions of Satire* (Baltimore: Johns Hopkins University Press, 1967), 181.

ditions of war—"Cannons, Culverins, Muskets. . . Sieges, Retreats, Attacks. . . dying Groans. . . Ravishing, Burning and
Destroying" (ii:247)—Gulliver concludes: "And, to set forth
the Valour of my own dear Countrymen, I assured him, that I
had seen them blow up a Hundred Enemies at once in a Siege,
and as many in a Ship; and beheld the dead Bodies drop down
in Pieces from the Clouds, to the great Diversion of all the
Spectators" (ii:247). Gulliver's discourse has obviously shifted
to direct satire.

The shift in technique is abrupt enough to require an explanation, which is given at the beginning of chapter 7: "The
Reader may be disposed to wonder how I could prevail on my
self to give so free a Representation of my own Species, Among
a Race of Mortals who were already too apt to conceive the
vilest Opinion of Human Kind, from the entire Congruity be-
twixt me and their *Yahoos*" (ii:258). Gulliver gives three explanations of his change: (1) association with the Houyhnhnms
has given him a low opinion of people; (2) the Houyhnhnm example has made him love truth; (3) he could not have hood-
winked his master anyway (ii:258). But when writing for us
now, Gulliver finds it "some Comfort to reflect, that in what I
said of my Countrymen, I *extenuated* their Faults as much as I
durst before so strict an Examiner; and upon every Article,
gave as *favourable* a Turn as the Matter would bear" (ii:258–95).
In this remark the satirist who is writing tells us that we are
worse than he has represented us to the Houyhnhnm. But Gulliver also reveals that he was even then concerned for his position in Houyhnhnmland. He did not wish to have his race
convicted of brutalities as bad as, or worse than, those of the
Yahoos.

Gulliver's account of war, however, ends in a comment that
cannot be represented as giving a favorable turn to human behavior: "Dead Bodies drop down in Pieces from the Clouds, to
the great Diversion of all the Spectators" (ii:247). This final remark is less effective satire than the catalog of brutalities leading up to it: it seems rather obviously to be exaggeratedly
satiric, perhaps producing a smile at the satirist more easily
than provoking a stern view of humanity. Although historically

people have responded with such levity to butchery, the observation cannot bear the weight of typicality that Gulliver places on it. We may recall that the King of Brobdingnag had been especially incensed because Gulliver in his description of war appeared "wholly unmoved at all the Scenes of Blood and Desolation" (II:135). This time Gulliver describes spectators so callous and bloodthirsty that there is no danger of identifying him with their evil. These spectators represent externally the hardhearted and violent imagination for which Gulliver has been rebuked. Stripped of the secret of his clothes, identified with the Yahoos whom he loathes, Gulliver assumes the garb of the satirist. If he gives a sufficiently vivid picture of the viciousness of his people, he will distinguish himself from them.[6]

Despite Gulliver's defensive use of literary convention, he insists on the literality of his story, contrasting it with other fictions. The frontispiece for Faulkner's 1735 edition of the *Travels* gives Gulliver the legend "Splendide Mendax," gloriously false, an epithet appropriate to Gulliver but in conflict with his claims. The tribute is taken from Horace's Odes (III, ii), and its specific context is the story of Danaus's daughters, one of whom was "gloriously false" to the unjust request of her father: unlike her sisters, she refused to kill her husband. The ode, an adjuration to Lyde not to scorn men, begins with an

[6]One tradition in the interpretation of satire refuses to acknowledge any element that does not have a polemical point; e.g., Sheldon Sacks, *Fiction and the Shape of Belief: A Study of Henry Fielding with Glances at Swift, Johnson, and Richardson* (Berkeley: University of California Press, 1964), subordinates all elements of a literary work to the function that Sacks defines for it: "A satire is a work organized so that it ridicules objects external to the fictional world created in it" (p. 26). Consequently "none of the fictional creations in *Gulliver's Travels* can ever themselves be satirized. . . . Similarly, any virtues which attach to the fictional creations within the book can be understood only as traits which enable Swift to maximize the ridicule directed at the external world" (pp. 7–8). Ronald Paulson's less schematic views seem to me more consistent with the development of eighteenth-century satire. In *The Fictions of Satire*, Paulson argues that "the typical satire of the Swift period . . . is specifically a fictional construct, both in the sense that it pretends to be something it is not, and in the sense that it produces stories, plots, and character relationships. This is the satire . . . that points the way to, and gradually merges into, the satiric novels of Fielding, Smollet, and Sterne, in which the representational qualities appear in a new relationship with the rhetorical" (pp. 8–9).

extended praise of the lyre, a tribute to the powers of the poet. Gulliver is "Splendide Mendax" in the sense that in order to fulfill a higher moral commitment he produces fiction. And his story has the traditional powers of song to transcend nature. Nevertheless, he refuses to fulfill the role of poet who does not lie because he does not pretend to truth, somewhat improbably preferring Dampier, the writer of travel books, as his literary antecedent. He insists that his truth is literal.[7]

For Gulliver fiction is falsehood. In the prefatory letter added to the 1735 edition of the *Travels*, he rejects the "Yahoo" contention that the *Travels* are "meer Fiction" and that "the *Houyhnhnms* and *Yahoos* have no more Existence than the Inhabitants of *Utopia*" (II:8). But the moral aim that Gulliver asserts for his writing links it to utopian literature, not to the reporting of travels: "A traveller's chief Aim should be to make Men wiser and better, and to improve their Minds by the bad, as well as the good Example of what they deliver concerning foreign Places" (II:291). Here Gulliver is attempting to link the assumedly literal travel book to the moral relevance of utopian fiction. Although Utopia, the good place, is nowhere, it is still a comment on us.[8]

As R. C. Elliott writes of Gulliver: "No traveler has ever had more experience of utopian modes of life than he. He explores not one but many utopias, some of these in such depth

[7]Michael Seidel, *Satiric Inheritance: Rabelais to Sterne* (Princeton: Princeton University Press, 1979), remarks, "One of the first indications of generic subversion in satiric literature is the claim of truth as a narrative privilege. . . .to insist that what any intelligent reader perceives as a fictional construct is indeed an historical record is to make the very issue of authority or 'legitimacy' part of the fictional subject at hand" (p. 61).

[8]Robert M. Philmus, "Swift, Gulliver, and 'The Thing Which Was Not,' " *ELH: A Journal of English Literary History* 38 (1971), 62-79, analyzes Gulliver's failure to understand the relationship between indirection and truth: "His Puritanical fixation on directness precludes his recognizing that, outside the confines of Houyhnhnmland, indirection, one paradigmatic mode of which is irony (in a way a species of circumlocution), accords with the nature of truthtelling" (p. 72). Philmus finds that Gulliver's "comic madness has its ultimate origin in the supposition that in a world degenerated from the aboriginal, or Edenic, harmony of logos—and the identity of the nominal and the real—he can still practice the Houyhnhnms' notion of how to communicate truth" (p. 79).

that he can report on utopias within utopias, as though he were following the idea back as far as he could trace it."[9] The first utopia that Gulliver describes is one that exists only in his imagining of a prior state of the Lilliputians: "In relating these and the following Laws, I would only be understood to mean the original Institutions, and not the most scandalous Corruptions into which these People are fallen by the degenerate Nature of Man" (II:60). In the next voyage Gulliver is given a lesson on how to disassemble the utopian vision. Gulliver describes a utopian version of England, including its House of Commons, "who were all principal Gentlemen, *freely* picked and culled out by the People themselves, for their great Abilities, and Love of their Country, to represent the Wisdom of the whole Nation" (II:128). The King wonders how these glittering words survive the strains of human nature: "How it came to pass, that People were so violently bent upon getting into this Assembly, which I allowed to be a great Trouble and Expence, often to the Ruin of their Families, without any Salary or Pension: Because this appeared such an exalted Strain of Virtue and publick Spirit, that his Majesty seemed to doubt it might possibly not be always sincere" (II:129-30). The King's persistent questions destroy the English utopia that Gulliver imagines. In the interstices of Gulliver's laudation, the King inserts the probabilities of human behavior, making an impassible barrier between Gulliver's words and English deeds.

The *Travels* provides a resolution of the issues that Thomas More raises in the prototypical *Utopia*. In part I, More and Hythloday articulate contrasting perspectives on the possibility of social improvement. More believes that "it is impossible that all should be well unless all men were good, a situation which I do not expect for a great many years to come."[10] In contrast, Hythloday derives man's evils from the social order:

[9]R. C. Elliott, *The Shape of Utopia: Studies in a Literary Genre* (Chicago: University of Chicago Press, 1970), 531.

[10]*Utopia*, ed. and trans. Edward Surtz, S.J. (New Haven: Yale University Press, 1964), 50. Brian Vickers, "The Satiric Structure of *Gulliver's Travels* and More's *Utopia,*" in *The World of Jonathan Swift*, ed. Brian Vickers (Oxford: Basil Blackwell, 1968), 250, comments on similarities between Gulliver and Hythloday, among them the methods used in their naming.

men steal because of need, and society creates need. If society were reorganized, it would be unnecessary for it to hang the thieves that it has made (pp. 27–28). These conflicting views of More and Hythloday provide the questioning frame for the account of Utopia: to what degree is it a Lucianic fantastic voyage, as suggested by the names (Hythloday, "well-learned in nonsense"), or an alternative to an admittedly corrupt society, as suggested by its verisimilitude? Gulliver's narrative supports the vision of More, the character in *Utopia,* and provides commentary that disassembles the utopia proposed by Hythloday.

The Brobdingnagian state is, from Gulliver's final point of view, the "least corrupted" of Yahoo nations, "whose wise Maxims in Morality and Government it would be our Happiness to observe" (II:292). But Gulliver also amply documents the insensitivity, greed, and malice of these people. Brobdingnag is a utopia in the negative sense that its institutions are not a source of additional corruption. But Gulliver, having learned from the King how to question utopian generalizations, is able to disinter the underside of the institutions of even this country:

> I was curious to know how this Prince, to whose Dominions there is no Access from any other Country, came to think of Armies, or to teach his People the Practice of military Discipline. But I was soon informed, both by Conversation, and Reading their Histories. For, in the Course of many Ages they have been troubled with the same Disease, to which the whole Race of Mankind is Subject; the Nobility often contending for Power, the People for Liberty, and the King for absolute Dominion. All which, however happily tempered by the Laws of that Kingdom, have been sometimes violated by each of the three Parties; and have more than once occasioned Civil Wars, the last whereof was happily put an End to by this Prince's Grandfather in a general Composition; and the Militia then settled with common Consent hath been ever since kept in the strictest Duty. [II:138]

In the third voyage, Gulliver depicts himself as visitor to an antiutopia. The attack on utopia is here extended to include the coerciveness of utopianizers, their desires to impose their fantasies on others, an explicit version of what is already implicit in More. The priests of *Utopia* "take the greatest pains from the very first to instill into children's minds, while still tender and pliable, good opinions, which are also useful for the preservation of their commonwealth" (*Utopia*, p. 140). These same priests "exclude from divine services persons whom they find to be unusually bad," and if such persons "do not demonstrate to the priests their speedy repentance, they are seized and punished by the senate for their impiety" (p. 140). The drive for conformity extends from the priests to society at large: "Being under the eyes of all, people are bound either to be performing the usual labor or to be enjoying their leisure in a fashion not without decency" (p. 83). Even the time of sleeping is uniform—eight hours (p. 70). What becomes apparent is the workings of a utopianizing mind: if one thing is better than another, then all should be the best, that is, similar. The very island of Utopia is given the shape that is best for its inhabitants (p. 59). What starts as an idea for eliminating the incentives to evil ends as an account of the details, sometimes minute, of one man's version of the good life. Decorum perhaps prevented a description of ideal toilet habits.

In the third voyage of the *Travels,* the utopianizing mind imposes its limited patterns on everything else, without regard to resistance or to lack of practical success. Its object is not the comprehension of nature but the subjection of all else to the patterns of the conceiving mind. As Martin Price remarks: "The Flying Island...is a world of pure self-indulgence, but it is also an instrument of power sought for its own sake."[11] The island is used to keep the sun and rain from rebellious communities, and (in the paragraphs at the end of chapter 3, which are omitted from early editions) it plays the part of England in op-

[11]Martin Price, *Swift's Rhetorical Art* (New Haven: Yale University Press, 1953), 83. The satire of the third voyage is, in fact, very broad, not narrowly focused on science. Pat Rogers, "Gulliver and the Engineers," *Modern Language Review* 70 (1975), 260–70, makes the point that commercial ventures are as much the background of the satire in the third voyage as are intellectual issues: "The best location for sources and analogues, as far as projects go, is not the *Philosophical Transactions* but the columns of newspapers in the Bubble era and the patent applications of the day" (p. 261).

pressing Dublin (Lindalino). Gulliver's patron, Lord Munodi, has already incurred the displeasure of the king for maintaining the old regularities despite modern scientific methods, and he fears he may have to destroy his magnificent holdings to avoid the "Censure of Pride, Singularity, Affectation, Ignorance, Caprice: and perhaps encrease his Majesty's Displeasure" (II:176). The Academy of Projectors on Balnibarbi too is coercive, "driven equally on by Hope and Despair" (II:177); failure merely increases the projectors' adamancy.

The Houyhnhnm society of the fourth voyage is pastoral, not centrally utopian.[12] These horses accommodate themselves to the patterns of nature rather than trying to subdue them. According to Gulliver, Houyhnhnm signifies etymologically "the *Perfection of Nature*" (II:235). Death causes the Houyhnhnms neither joy nor grief and is described by a word that Gulliver renders into English as "to retire to his first Mother" (II: 275). In their attitude to nature they contrast sharply to the Laputans, who impose the shapes of their obsessions even on their food: "a shoulder of Mutton, cut into an Aequilateral Triangle. . . , Sausages and Puddings resembling Flutes and Hautboys" (II:161). The astronomy of the Houyhnhnms permits them to calculate years and to "understand the Nature of Eclipses" (II:273), a practical and calming use of their knowledge of nature; whereas the Laputans are terrified by the potential disasters uncovered by their astronomy.

This fourth voyage of the *Travels* extends the analysis of utopia until both primitivist and Hobbesian versions of society are scrutinized. Gulliver's Houyhnhnm master adopts Montaigne's primitivist view of the failings of European civilization. For both Montaigne and the Houyhnhnm, the human

[12]Martin Price, in *To the Palace of Wisdom: Studies in Order and Energy from Dryden to Blake* (Garden City: Doubleday, 1964), remarks: "In the land of the Houyhnhnms, we find an anarchy of reasonable creatures, such as William Godwin admired. The rational horses need no government; they immediately intuit their duties and perform them" (p. 200). Northrop Frye, *The Stubborn Structure: Essays on Criticism and Society* (Ithaca: Cornell University Press, 1970), finds the "conception of the ideal society as simplified, even primitive," to be pastoral rather than centrally utopian (p. 125). He categorizes the fourth voyage of the *Travels* as "pastoral satire" (p. 128).

version of reason creates social structures that aggravate rather than ameliorate evils. And Gulliver applies Montaigne's view of happy savages to the Houyhnhnms, even using language quite similar to Montaigne's (see II:273–77). In "Of Cannibals," Montaigne describes a happily savage society as a "nation wherein there is no manner of traffic, no knowledge of letters, no science of numbers, no name of magistrate or political superiority; no use of service, riches or poverty, no contracts, no successions, no dividends, no properties, no employments, but those of leisure, no respect of kindred, but common, no clothing, no agriculture, no metal, no use of corn or wine; the very words that signify lying, treachery, dissimulation, avarice, envy, detraction, pardon, never heard of."[13] Montaigne suggests that such a nation is close to its "original simplicity" and is still ruled by "laws of nature...not as yet much vitiated with any mixture of ours" (p. 93). He expresses a belief that the actuality of such a primitive society exceeds what the poets have imaginatively attributed to a golden age (pp. 93–94). In the "Apology of Raymond Sebond," too, Montaigne envisions an idyllic existence among the Brazilians. He regards the peace of their physical lives as evidence of the mental peace that is possible when European learning is banished: "That they never die but of old age, is attributed to the serenity and tranquillity of the air they live in; but I attribute it to the serenity and tranquillity of their soul, free from all passion, thought, or employments, continuous or unpleasing, as people that pass over their lives in an admirable simplicity and ignorance, without letters, without law, without king, or any manner of religion" (p. 235).

But Montaigne's primitivism is refuted by the fable of the fourth voyage.[14] The Yahoos, not the Houyhnhnms, are repre-

[13]*The Essays of Michel Eyquem de Montaigne,* trans. Charles Cotton, ed. W. Carew Hazlitt (Chicago: Encyclopaedia Britannica, 1952), 94.

[14]T. O. Wedel, "On the Philosophical Background of *Gulliver's Travels,*" *Studies in Philology* 23 (1926), 446–47, finds that "the best commentary on *Gulliver's Travels* is the great *Apologie de Raymond Sebonde*" (p. 446). Wedel emphasizes the "attack upon Stoic pride" in Montaigne and Swift but recognizes that the primitivism of Montaigne is not easily reconciled with what Wedel also calls the "primitivism" of Swift (p. 446). Wedel notes that the Yahoos are

sentative of people in nature without the distortions of culture. They have indeed not complicated and institutionalized their viciousness to the degree that Europeans have, but, as Gulliver's master recognizes, they are hardly an idealized version of Gulliver: "The two *Yahoos* said to be first seen among them, had been driven thither over the Sea. . . . being forsaken by their Companions, they retired to the Mountains, and degenerating by Degrees, became in Process of Time, much more savage than those of their own Species in the Country from whence these two Originals came. The Reason of his Assertion was, that he had now in his Possession, a certain wonderful *Yahoo*, (meaning myself) which most of them had heard of, and many of them had seen" (II:272). The view of humanity implied by this myth of the origins of the Yahoos can in a limited sense be called Hobbesian: in the state of nature life is "solitary, poore, nasty, brutish, and short" (*Leviathan*, I, 13, p. 186). Although neither Gulliver's master nor Gulliver is willing to praise European culture, it is apparent that the Yahoos represent a degeneration that is facilitated by the absence of society.

In contrast to Hobbes's view, the culture of the Houyhnhnms reflects their virtue but does not cause it. According to Hobbes, people can leave this brutish state of nature only when they give up certain of their rights to a sovereign, who compels them to obey. The Houyhnhnms, however, "have no Conception how a rational Creature can be *compelled*" (II:280). They are governed by reason and nature, not by laws.

In Swift's fable then, the Yahoos implicitly contradict Montaigne's vision of the possibility of an idyllic life free from human law, and the Houyhnhnms counter Hobbes's assertion that the good life is to be found only in an order that preempts the order of nature. These sharp contradictions between two versions of society require some more comprehensive scheme for their reconciliation than that of either Montaigne or Hobbes, Gulliver or Houyhnhnm. Although the Houyhnhnms

---

in Hobbes's state of nature and speculates that the Houyhnhnms may represent Locke's version of the state of nature. In the *Travels*, however, "Swift is clearly neither Hobbes nor Locke" (p. 443).

are an example of goodness as compared to the Yahoos, it does not follow that their conceptions of the Yahoos or of people are necessarily adequate. Indeed, the very goodness of the Houyhnhnms makes them unable to comprehend certain complexities of human perversion.

A comparison of the Houyhnhnms to More's Utopians may serve to emphasize some of the limitations and advantages of Swift's horses. Both the Utopians and Houyhnhnms accept nature as normative. Utopian "nature" calls all people to seek pleasure for themselves and, as a consequence, for others. They must carefully order a society to maximize the pleasures of all. But Gulliver's Houyhnhnm master cannot even comprehend what Gulliver means by "*Law* and the Dispensers thereof," because "Nature and Reason" are "sufficient Guides" for him (ii:248). Furthermore, Utopian pleasure seeking eventually leads to religion, as the ultimate pleasure is that of the "immense and never-ending gladness" given by God (*Utopia*, p. 194). But Houyhnhnm discussions of "the visible Operations of Nature" do not appear to lead to a conception of a law above nature's law (ii:277).[15]

Both More and Swift are presenting societies that have not been Christianized, societies whose only revelation is from nature and reason. But Swift's creatures are confined within nature. Although they have an unvarying virtue that More's Utopians lack, their reason does not lead to the divine. Because of their goodness, they cannot (and need not) understand the function of positive law, and because of their naturalism, they are oblivious to the connections of law to the divine.

Gulliver's program of literalism makes it difficult for him to place either the Houyhnhnms or his own society in any larger scheme. He perceives Houyhnhnm goodness but not how it might be effectually related to human society. Having rejected all fictions, he is unable to link the ideal and the real. Seeing the failure of human institutions to produce utopia, Gulliver rejects all institutions and commits himself to the one example

[15]In this respect I now differ with my "Gulliver the Preacher," *PLMA* 89 (1974), 1026.

of goodness that he has found—the Houyhnhnms' pastoral existence. Although this goodness does not result from a program, Gulliver attempts to impose the Houyhnhnms' characteristics on himself and on others. In addition to appropriately imitating Houyhnhnm virtues, Gulliver tries to gallop and neigh.

Richard Hooker wrote *Of the Laws of Ecclesiastical Polity* to combat a vision similar to Gulliver's. He confronts the literalistic argument of the Puritans that human institutions are corrupt and corrupting unless explicitly sanctioned in the Bible. (Gulliver treats Houyhnhnm society as his bible.) But while acknowledging human corruption, Hooker also links the institutions that people have created to the divine, arguing that God expects people to use their divinely implanted reason to create institutions that will limit evil and will promote good. Hooker acknowledges the absence of utopia without as a consequence denying the efficacy of institutions.

Hooker's conception of law, derived from St. Thomas, is far more inclusive than the Houyhnhnms' and contrasts sharply with Gulliver's: "Of Law there can be no less acknowledged, than that her seat is the bosom of God, her voice the harmony of the world."[16] Unlike the Houyhnhnms, Hooker distinguishes many kinds of law, all of which are related and all of which ultimately come from God. Included among Hooker's definitions of law are the following: (1) external law: the law "laid up in the bosom of God" (2) natural law: "that part of it which ordereth natural agents" (3) human law: "that which out of the law either of reason or God men probably gathering to be expedient, they make it a law" (pp. 154–55). The Houyhnhnms conceive of the laws of nature and of reason, but not of external, divine, or human law. Hooker's answer to the Houyhnhnms' incomprehension of human law is that "the corruption of our nature being presupposed, we may not deny but that the Law of Nature doth now require of necessity some kind of regiment" (p. 191). The uncorrupted Houyhnhnms need no

---

[16]Richard Hooker, *Of the Laws of Ecclesiastical Polity,* Everyman ed. (New York: E. P. Dutton, 1925), 232.

such "regiment," but to deny it to man is to reduce him to savagery.

Following his conversion to the Houyhnhnms, Gulliver's analysis of human law suggests that it is only a contrivance to debase human existence. While this view fits many of the facts that Gulliver adduces, it ignores any possibility of improvement, any possibility that the conception of law may be imperfectly realized in his society. The analysis of utopian societies that is implied by Gulliver's experiences of the first voyage, and especially by those of the third voyage, does indeed support his belief that law, itself, can do little but organize the destructive potentialities of human societies more efficiently. But the Brobdingnagian society provides at least an understated counterview to this conception of law: the King of Brobdingnag "confined the Knowledge of governing within very *narrow Bounds*; to common sense and Reason, to Justice and Lenity, to the Speedy Determination of Civil and criminal Causes" (II:135).

Gulliver's horror of saying "the thing which is not" confines him to "the thing which is." Law, for example, is only its human manifestations. He rejects any multivalence. His insistence on the literality that he imputes to the travel book is part of a larger indifference to the connections of the human and divine. He follows the Houyhnhnms into nature and rejects the possibilities as well as the limitations of his being both animal and spirit.

Gulliver's refusal to notice the meanings of his clothes is a prominent example of his determined suppression of all but the literal. Martin Price remarks of the social symbolism of clothes in Swift: "The perfectly rational Houyhnhnms need no clothes; their bodies represent no challenge to their reason. For most men clothes are the necessary emblem of the *human* animal, the necessary restraint placed upon the passions of the body."[17] In the *Travels,* clothes imply both this social order and the religious conceptions on which it ought to be based. Kathleen Williams remarks on the connection between the

---

[17]Price, *Swift's Rhetorical Art,* 105.

symbolism of clothes and the fall of man: "The signification was an old one among Christian moralists, who inferred from Genesis that the urge to clothe ourselves is an urge to cover our nakedness both of body and mind, and a direct consequence of the Fall."[18] Clothes symbolize the social structures that we use to mitigate the degeneration consequent on the fall; they are also a tacit acknowledgment of the fall. In the fourth voyage of the *Travels,* clothes suggest, then, the fundamental issues that Hooker develops in connection with law: man's need for a social structure and the relationship of that structure to a divine order.

Gulliver's master interprets clothes according to his notion of the order of nature: "He could not understand why Nature should teach us to conceal what Nature had given" (II:237). From the Houyhnhnm's perspective, Gulliver's need of clothes to keep warm is, like the uselessness of his "claws," only evidence of his inferiority to other Yahoos. The only hierarchy the Houyhnhnm recognizes is limited to nature. For Gulliver to accept this doctrine is to fix himself forever as a Yahoo, to acquiesce in the loathsome condition of man. But Gulliver learns early in the fourth voyage that one of the uses of his clothes is to puzzle the horses, because his clothes make it more difficult for them to identify him absolutely with the naked Yahoos. Consequently when the secret of Gulliver's clothing is discovered, he requests of his master that "my having a false Covering to my Body might be known to none but himself" (II:237). Gulliver's clothes became a badge of his bad faith: he accepts the Houyhnhnm's view but wishes to conceal its relevance to himself.

The principal distinction between Gulliver and the Yahoos is, indeed, that which is represented by Gulliver's clothes. If the clothes are taken in their fullest symbolic sense, the distinction is great. That Gulliver has to replace his clothes with animal skins (II:276) suggests the story of man's fall and redemption. Adam and Eve clothe themselves in leaves to hide their shame; God then clothes them in skins, a figure of

---

[18]Kathleen Williams, *Jonathan Swift and the Age of Compromise* (Lawrence: University of Kansas Press, 1958), 183.

Christ's atonement for their sins; Gulliver, however, does not note this analogy. He has committed himself to systematic hypocrisy, and his clothes are an attempt at a denial of his fallen condition. Gulliver ignores even the simple social and moral restraints that are part of the meaning of clothes. When he once strips himself "stark naked," he is attacked by a female Yahoo "inflamed by Desire." Gulliver's "Mortification" is that he can "no longer deny, that I was a real *Yahoo,* in every limb and Feature" (II:266, 267). But he does not move from his own humiliation to a consideration of the human regulations that introduce an element of order into such encounters. Houyhnhnm sexuality is entirely self-controlled (these horses are as grave as the Shandy bull), but humans must have laws (and clothes) to restrain their impulses to unchastity.

Gulliver's experiences after he is exiled from Houyhnhnmland dramatize the anomaly of his position as a clothed primitivist. His first meeting with humans is with "stark naked" natives, who immediately attack and wound him (II:284). Gulliver flees but, seeing a sail, returns: "My Detestation of the *Yahoo* Race prevailed...choosing rather to trust my self among these *Barbarians,* than live with *European Yahoos*" (II:285). He has internalized a moral system that interprets civilization as necessarily corrupting. At the same time, he uses his clothes to differentiate himself from the Yahoos and savages who are the image of the corruption that he attributes to the entire human race. His "savage Dress" is for him a badge of a previous existence in which he had risen above his herd. In contrast the Europeans see that same dress as a sign of the distance he has traveled from civilization: "The Captain had often intreated me to strip myself of my savage Dress, and offered to lend me the best Suit of Cloathes he had. This I would not be prevailed on to accept, abhorring to cover myself with any thing that had been on the Back of a *Yahoo*" (II:288). Gulliver's reintegration into society begins when he gets a new suit. He has been measured for suits before—accurately in Lilliput, inaccurately in Laputa—but now he will not even "suffer the Taylor to take my Measure" (II:288). The suit fits anyway, however—"Don *Pedro* being almost of my Size"—and Gulliver must wear it.

In discussing the utopian and pastoral versions of the ideal society, Northrop Frye remarks on their biblical origins: "In Christianity the city is the form of the myth of Telos, the New Jerusalem that is the end of the human pilgrimage. But there is no city in the Christian, or Judeo-Christian, myth of origin: that has only a garden, and the two progenitors of what was clearly intended to be a simple and patriarchal society."[19] Rather than aspiring to the City of God, Gulliver wishes to return to Eden. Having rejected utopia, he compares human society not with what it might become but with the pastoral condition that preceded it. And he identifies himself as the only human visitor to that condition.

As I argued earlier, an emphasis on the meaning of the described scene moves the traveler's story toward utopia, and a concern with the traveler's responses moves it toward autobiography. Utopia fails to satisfy Gulliver's concern for literality, and autobiography his concern for objectivity. Nevertheless, a tendency toward autobiography is evident even in so factually organized a travel book as *A New Voyage Round the World*, the book Gulliver adopts as the prototype for his *Travels*. In theory Dampier subordinates his personal accounts to his presentation of geography and natural history: he describes "the particular traverses I made" in order that the reader will "acquiesce in my Description of Places."[20] And he describes the often scoundrelly actions of his fellow travelers neutrally, as if they had no integral relationship to his narrative. But Dampier eventually rejects the complicity implied by his neutral account and wishes to escape from this "mad Crew" (p. 277). His section on a series of storms culminates in this description of his repentance:

> But here I had a lingring View of approaching Death, and little or no hopes of escaping it; and I must confess that my Courage which I had hitherto kept up, failed me here; and I made very sad Reflections on my former Life, and looked back with Hor-

[19]Frye, *The Stubborn Structure*, 125.
[20]William Dampier, *A New Voyage Round the World* (London: Argonaut Press, 1927), 3.

rour and Detestation on Actions which before I disliked, but now
I trembled at the remembrance of. I had long before this re-
pented me of that roving Course of Life, but never with such
Concern as now. I did also call to mind the many miraculous
Acts of God's Providence towards me in the whole Course of my
Life, of which kind I believe few men have met with the like. For
all these I returned Thanks in a peculiar Manner, and thus once
more desired God's Assistance, and composed my Mind as well
as I could in the Hopes of it, and as the Event shew'd, I was not
disappointed of my Hopes. [Pp. 332-33]

The seeming externality of Dampier's account disappears, sub-
merged temporarily in the patterns characteristic of spiritual
autobiography.[21] The entire ending segment of Dampier's story
is more personal than the earlier portions, including commentary on his motivations and an account of his sickness.

Dampier accedes even more fully to the autobiographical
pressures on a travel book when in *Voyages and Discoveries,* published in 1699 (two years after the *new Voyage*), he includes a
brief summary of his life.[22] At the beginning of the "Voyage to
the Bay of Campeachy" he writes of his education, of his "first
going to Sea" (p. 108), and of the series of voyages that led up
to *A New Voyage Round the World*. Readers of *Robinson Crusoe* and
the *Travels* will particularly note Dampier's references to his
propensities for wandering, his "Inclinations of seeing the
World" (p. 108), his "growing weary of staying ashore" (p.
109), and his recovery of his "Old Inclination for the Sea" (p.
109).

Like Dampier, Gulliver acknowledges the demands of a travel book: "Having already lived three years in this Country,
the Reader I suppose will expect, that I should, like other Travellers, give him some Account of the Manners and Customs of

---

[21]Roger Sharrock defines spiritual autobiography in his introduction to
Bunyan's *Grace Abounding* (London: Clarendon Press, 1962). George Starr,
Defoe and Spiritual Autobiography (Princeton: Princeton University Press, 1965),
shows that "spiritual autobiography was the common property of English
Protestantism" (p. x).

[22]*Dampier's Voyages,* vol. 2, ed. John Masefield (New York: E. P. Dutton,
1906).

its Inhabitants, which it was indeed my principal Study to learn" (II:267). Furthermore, he rejects the drift toward autobiography: "This is enough to say upon the Subject of my Dyet, wherewith other Travellers fill their Books, as if the Readers were personally concerned, whether we fare well or ill" (II:232-33). But Gulliver in fact expands the autobiographical elements of the travel book enormously while in theory accepting the generic imperatives that Dampier states—suppress the self, but retain a thread of narrative to validate the story. Gulliver is his own topic much of the time.

Gulliver makes a series of autobiographical remarks, similar to Dampier's about his lust for travel, implying a pattern of continuing moral and psychological debilitation. He first travels to make money, but by the end of his first voyage, he has acquired an "insatiable Desire of seeing foreign Countries" (II:80). He characterizes his leaving again as the result of "having been condemned by Nature and Fortune to an active and restless Life" (II:83). After his second voyage, his "evil Destiny" drives him to leave again (II:149). He then goes on his third voyage, "the Thirst I had of seeing the World notwithstanding my past Misfortunes, continuing as violent as ever" (II:153-54). His fourth voyage results from not having "learned the Lesson of knowing when I was well" (II:221). This sequence of sea disasters is characteristic of "providence" literature, and even in a travel book Dampier interprets the storm and the saving of his life as a result of God's providential intervention.[23] "Providence" is not, however, Gulliver's mode of explanation. When shipwrecked in the first voyage, he and his companions trust themselves "to the Mercy of the Waves" (p. 21); and Gulliver subsequently swims as "Fortune" directs him. He finally leaves Blefuscu because, he tells the king, "Fortune, whether good or evil, had thrown a Vessel in my Way" (p. 77). So resolute a resistance to the expected reflections of a Christian on such occasions suggests at least the possibility that impiety will

[23]J. Paul Hunter, *The Reluctant Pilgrim: Defoe's Emblematic Method and Quest for Form in "Robinson Crusoe"* (Baltimore: Johns Hopkins University Press, 1966), discusses the conventions of "providence literature" (chap. 6).

be corrected.[24] But the fourth voyage gives us a vision that expresses no greater awareness of Providence. Gulliver's conception of goodness is there limited to the Houyhnhnms, and the Houyhnhnms are limited to the order of nature.

Gulliver shapes his story as if to lead to a chastening disaster, but when it comes, he sees the error of our ways more vividly than he sees the errors of his. The story of Gulliver's misunderstanding of himself is superimposed on the story of his understanding of mankind. Following the patterns of travel book and utopia, Gulliver defines mankind's monstrousness. But the autobiographical elements of his book implicate him in the evil that he sees. Nevertheless, in Houyhnhnmland and in Brobdingnag—the two societies that he uses to provide a standard for Europeans—Gulliver systematically avoids his own reflection. His final program of self-reformation includes his attempt "to behold my Figure often in a Glass, and thus if possible habituate my self in Time to tolerate the Sight of a human Creature" (II:295), but this program of attempted self-understanding is abortive, consisting of only a few abandoned

[24]Hugh Kenner, *The Counterfeiters: An Historical Comedy* (Bloomington: Indiana University Press, 1968), observes that Gulliver "lacks what the ancients called *pietas*" (p. 129). He slights familial responsibilities and "does not mention God, of whom he seems not to have heard" (ibid.). John J. McManmon, "The Problem of a Religious Interpretation of Gulliver's Fourth Voyage," *Journal of the History of Ideas* 27 (1966), 59–72, concludes: "It seems, then, that there is no internal evidence in *Gulliver IV* that its author was either a clergyman or a Christian. Thus, suspicion falls heavily on any attempt to use these two biographical facts as a basis for an interpretation of the Fourth Voyage" (p. 74). Similar skepticism about a "religious interpretation" has also been evidenced by other critics. I agree that studying a work from the hypothetical perspective of purely "internal evidence" may be heuristically useful. I do not find, however, that the removal of a work's language from its context (explicit or implicit) is an adequately comprehensive, or even possible, method of interpretation. Gulliver refuses to trample the cross at the end of the third voyage, he identifies himself as an Englishman who was educated at Cambridge, and his voyages begin in 1699. Swift's, or any European author's, exclusion of Christianity from the world view of such a character, believer or nonbeliever, is noteworthy. The phrase "religious interpretation" is, of course, ambiguous. In a broad sense, it seems difficult for anyone to avoid a "religious interpretation" of the *Travels;* it also seems difficult for anyone entirely to assimilate the *Travels* to a narrowly conceived religious function.

gestures near the end of the book. He turns from self-observation to an insistence on his lofty position outside society: "I dwell the longer upon this Subject [pride] from the Desire I have to make the Society of an *English Yahoo* by any Means not unsupportable; and therefore I here intreat those who have any Tincture of this absurd Vice, that they will not presume to appear in my Sight" (II:296). Gulliver finally uses his book—his excoriation of mankind—as a defense against his perceptions of himself. He struggles to avoid seeing himself in a pond, a mirror, or a book. Gulliver's insistence that his book is a univocal record of literal events continues even as it becomes increasingly apparent that it is a compendium of fictions.[25] Instead of a literal representation of truth—unfictionality—Gulliver gives us another level of fiction that articulates not only his vision of the world but also his attempts to suppress his implication in that world.

[25]Jenny Mezciems, "Gulliver and Other Heroes," in *The Art of Jonathan Swift*, ed. Clive T. Probyn (New York: Barnes and Noble, 1978), 189–208, notes that many literary figures lie behind Gulliver: "It is by means of the barriers between him and a range of figures at various imprecisely measured distances from him, this penumbra of shadowy allusions which causes his silhouette to fade in and out of an uncertain outline, that Swift obliges us to take Gulliver so seriously as he does himself" (p. 205).

CHAPTER 6

The Language of Self

Unlike the narrator of the *Tale,* whose goal is polysemousness, Gulliver suppresses the reverberations of his words in the interest of the univocal literal; he must leave no room for the "thing which is not," that is, fiction. While Swift provides many signs of the multivalency of the narrative, Gulliver asserts that his book is a record of literal events. Choosing the travel book as the form for his story, Gulliver adopts the convention that what he is describing is divorced from any private concerns of the speaker. This convention is one that the satirist often adopts: satirists only describe what people do. But Swift makes Gulliver's satiric pose transparent by revealing the process of its development. He derives Gulliver's final satiric style from his early objective "Royal Society" style, showing the attitudes to human behavior that were espoused by the new scientists being adapted to the ulterior purposes of the moralizing satirist. Gulliver exemplifies Swift's remark in "Thoughts on Religion" that "violent zeal for truth hath an hundred to one odds to be either petulancy, ambition, or pride" (9:261).

From its early days the Royal Society attempted to define an ideal of style. Members of the Society discerned two problems in the use of language. First, the writer might not be clearly understood; consequently a simple style and vocabulary were enjoined. Second, the writer might mislead the audience because of a confusion between the subject matter being described and the writer's private interpretations of the subject matter; consequently, fact and conjecture were to be sharply separated. Reflected in these stylistic concerns of the Society is a belief that human subjectivity is an obstacle to truth that can and should be overcome. In this suspicion of subjectivity, the Society follows Bacon, whose definitions in the *Novum Organum* of the "Idols" that hinder human understanding are an account of the categories of distortion that lead a human being to attribute truth to a purely private vision. The "Idols of the Tribe" are the consequence of being human and therefore of having a peculiar perspective on the remainder of nature; the "Idols of the Cave" are the consequence of being an individual who imposes even private peculiarities on all else; the "Idols of the Marketplace" are the consequence of having a linguistic system that imposes its own fixities and laxities on whatever is communicated; and the "Idols of the Theater" are the consequence of those systems of thought that infiltrate the human mind and compromise its observations.

In the Royal Society's original statutes of 1663, the following injunctions are included in chapter 5 ("Of Experiments and the Reports thereof"):

Two or more Curators shall be appointed (if it may consist with convenience) of every Experiment, or natural Observation, that cannot conveniently be made in the presence of the Society. . . . if any difference shall happen between them in their apprehensions thereabout, the same shall be related in the Report.

In all Reports of Experiments to be brought into the Society, the Matter of fact shall be barely stated, without any prefaces, apologies, or rhetorical flourishes; and entered so in the Register book, by order of the Society. And if any Fellow shall think fit to suggest any conjecture, concerning the causes of the phaenomena in such Experiments, the same shall be done apart.[1]

The purpose of these statutes is to make possible a report that will provide the reader with the same benefits that were af-

[1] *The Record of the Royal Society of London for the Promotion of Natural Knowledge*, 4th ed. (Edinburgh: Morrison and Gibb, 1940), 289-90.

forded to the experimenter. This use of language is epistemological—intended to be truth in itself and, consequently, a step toward the next truth.[2]

A. C. Howell discusses the apparently related conception of "Res et Verba" in the seventeenth century.[3] The tendency in the later part of the century (but going back to Bacon and further to Quintilian) was to denigrate any stylistic trait that distracted the reader from the subject matter. But, Howell suggests, "res" became associated not just with subject matter but with, literally, things: "The tendency to assume that *things* should be expressible in *words,* or conversely, *words* should represent *things,* not metaphysical and abstract concepts, may be discerned" (Howell, p. 131). Sprat's often-quoted norm for style, "when men deliver'd so many *things,* almost in an equal number of *words,* " has as its function the facilitation of the Society's intention "to heap up a mixt Mass of Experiments": "The *Society* has reduc'd its principal observations, into one *common-stock;* and laid them up in publique *Registers,* to be nakedly transmitted to the next Generation of Men; and so from them, to their Successors."[4] The words have in Sprat's language become the experiments. Because this use of language reifies and stabilizes the experiments, they can now be heaped and moved.

As R. W. Frantz has shown, the Royal Society's requests for information and definitions of procedures for acquiring it influenced much of the travel literature of the late seventeenth and early eighteenth centuries in both form and content.[5] Dam-

[2]James Knowlson, *Universal Language Schemes in England and France, 1600–1800* (Toronto: University of Toronto Press, 1975), discusses the conception that underlay some attempts at a "real character": "learning and using the philosophical language would be the linguistic equivalent of learning and using real knowledge" (p. 97).

[3]A. C. Howell, "Res et Verba: Words and Things," *ELH: A Journal of English Literary History* 13 (1946), 131–42.

[4]Thomas Sprat, *History of the Royal Society,* ed. Jackson I. Cope and Harold Whitmore Jones, Washington University Studies (St. Louis: Washington University, 1958), 113, 115.

[5]R. W. Frantz, *The English Traveller and the Movement of Ideas, 1660–1732* (Lincoln: University of Nebraska Press, 1934), chaps. 1, 2.

pier's work, in particular, reflects not only the specific desires of the Royal Society for certain categories of information but also the attitudes evidenced in the Royal Society's stylistic program.[6] Dampier includes personal accounts to testify to his actually having observed what he describes, but he limits such accounts because he wishes to be "particular," to accumulate as much information about externalities as possible. Like the experimenters, he gives his own observations without comparing them to other accounts: "In differing Accounts, even of the same things, it can hardly be but there will be some new Light afforded by each of them" (p. 3.) Dampier's book (dedicated to Charles Montagu, president of the Royal Society) reveals the same conception of the distorting effects of subjectivity and the same confidence in the possibility of surmounting it that we find in the Royal Society statutes. He wishes to avoid contaminating his observations by relying on other minds or by intruding his personal concerns. Despite the inevitable limitations of any observer, he implies that the unprejudiced accounts of all witnesses will lead to some larger truth.

Gulliver too is concerned to defend the validity of his observations: he even brings back artifacts. And like the Royal Society and Dampier, he is concerned to make a distinction between the objective and the subjective. Gulliver's description of his shipwreck and landing in Lilliput illustrates a resolute attempt to separate the personal and private from the externally verifiable and to give the factual basis for each hypothesis. "What became of my Companions in the Boat, as well as of those who escaped on the Rock, or were left in the Vessel, I cannot tell; but conclude they were all lost" (II: 21): he separates his conclusion from what he has actually observed. The time of his arrival on shore is not just "about Eight O'Clock": Gulliver precedes his announcement of an approximate time with "I conjectured," emphasizing the subjectivity of the process of arriving at the information. He finds no inhabitants but remarks on his awareness of his own deficiencies as an observer:

---

[6]See William Dampier's preface to *A New Voyage Round the World* (London: Argonaut Press, 1927).

"At least I was in so weak a Condition, that I did not observe them." He does not merely assert his sleepiness but validates its probability on the basis of physical causes: he is tired and hot and had drunk half a pint of brandy. He awakens "as I reckoned, above Nine hours" later. How does he know? "For when I awaked, it was just Day-light."

The effect of Gulliver's procedures is, however, markedly different from that of his "Cousin" Dampier's. The most notable aspect of Gulliver's description is what is absent from it. There is no expression of fear when he drops his legs "and could feel no Bottom" (II:21) and no rejoicing when, "almost gone, and able to struggle no longer," he finds himself able to wade. Gulliver is an actor in this passage and only secondarily an observer, yet he appears almost ostentatiously as a processor and producer of information that is not especially relevent to the central issue of this passage—his survival. The effect implies emotional suppression rather than accurate reporting alone. Despite his evident attention to numbering and measuring, Gulliver's method of description elsewhere also calls attention to his empathy with the scenes that he describes. His device for measuring a cancer in the second voyage, for example, is involving, not distancing: "There was a Woman with a Cancer in her Breast, swelled to a monstrous Size, full of Holes, in two or three of which I could have easily crept, and covered my whole Body" (II:112–13).

Swift manages to suggest that an objective style may be a not entirely successful attempt to mask the emotional involvement of the perceiver. In order to isolate and emphasize some of the characteristics of Swift's descriptive method, it may be helpful to examine three versions of a dog's suffering: as exhibited in a Royal Society experiment, in the third voyage of the *Travels,* and in Hogarth's *Four Stages of Cruelty.*

In his *History,* Sprat includes among selected other papers of the Royal Society "An Account of a Dog dissected. By Mr. Hook."

In prosecution of some Inquiries into the Nature of Respiration in several Animals; a Dog was dissected, and by means of a pair of bellows, and a certain Pipe thrust into the Wind-pipe of the Creature, the heart continued beating for a very long while after all the thorax and Belly had been open'd, nay after the *Diaphragme* had been in a great part cut away, and the *Pericardium* remov'd from the heart. . . .though we found, that upon removing the Bellows, the Lungs would presently grow flaccid, and the Heart begin to have convulsive motions; but upon removing [*sic;* renewing?] the motion of the Bellows, the Heart recovered its former motion, and the Convulsions ceased. Though I made a *Ligature* upon all the great Vessels that went into the lower parts of its Body, I could not find any alteration in the pulse of the Heart; the circulation, it seems, being perform'd some other way. [P. 232]

The grave, businesslike style rather effectively objectifies the dog, although its tissues perhaps remind us too much of our own for the description to leave at least the novice experimenter entirely at ease.

The dog that appears in Swift is also the subject of an operation by a bellows. This bellows, however, has "a long slender Muzzle of Ivory," which is "conveyed eight Inches up the Anus" (II:181), a location perhaps even more difficult to regard dispassionately than the thorax. After the neutrally described operation, the dog produces a "Discharge, as was very offensive to me and my Companions." The offense is futile, unredeemed by any beneficent consequence: "The Dog died on the Spot, and we left the Doctor endeavouring to recover him by the same Operation." The mention of an offensive discharge destroys the impassivity of the passage: a dog who moves us to respond to his stink may also move us to respond to his pain. But the passage, even before the offensive discharge, could hardly evoke the neutral response that its language seems to imply. The operation is described and is then shown to Gulliver after he complains "of a small fit of the Cholick; upon which my Conductor led me into a Room, where a great Physician resided, who was famous for curing that Disease" (II:181). The dog is throughout regarded as a substitute for, and as an analogy to, Gulliver.

The fourth plate of Hogarth's *Four Stages of Cruelty*, "The Re-

ward of Cruelty," presents simultaneously the complexities of
attitude that appear in Swift's narrative. Scientific objectivity,
callous indifference, and a lust for cruelty are all shown in the
faces of the spectators and participants at an anatomy demonstration. The central seated figure impassively gives the demonstration as his assistants (one of them with considerable
enthusiasm) carve up the hanged Tom Nero. As most of the
spectators are engaged in matters unrelated to the demonstration, it is of little or no instructional importance. Hogarth jux-
taposes a spectrum of cruelties from the socially acceptable one
of pretended scientific curiosity, through indifference, to ma-
levolence. Furthermore, these images are connected in narrative fashion with recollections of the first plate that revivify the
dead man, making our nerves, if not his, quiver. The pretense
of abstracted propriety in the fourth plate is violently disturbed
by a dog that gnaws on Tom Nero's heart. In the center of the
first plate Tom Nero is thrusting an arrow into an anguished
dog's anus. In the fourth plate, an assistant gouges out Tom
Nero's eye, and in the first plate, the eye of a live bird is being
burned out. In the upper corner of the first plate, a bit of scientific curiosity presides over the whole scene—a cat with wings
attached is tossed out of an upper-story window.

Such inspiriting of the seemingly objective with the intensely, and not always savory, subjective is amply exemplified
in the *Travels*. Gulliver's epistemologically motivated attempt to
separate the subjective from the objective early in the *Travels*
becomes a method for both defining and insulating a vulnera-
ble self in the second voyage. As a defense against his fears and
humiliations among the giants, Gulliver moves closer to his final detachment: "As I was not in a Condition to resent In-
juries, so, upon mature Thoughts, I began to doubt whether I
were injured or no" (II:107). One of the pains of Brobdingnag
for Gulliver is seeing his own physicality enlarged and the behavior of his kind vehemently replicated. Although he "ab-
horred such Kind of Spectacles," he witnesses an execution:
"The Veins and Arteries spouted up such a prodigious Quantity of Blood, and so high in the Air, that the great *Jet d'Eau* at
Versailles was not equal for the Time it lasted" (II:119, 120). Gul-

liver's choice of metaphor turns the grisly spectacle into an inanimate European one. Here as elsewhere Gulliver keeps his magnified vision of the giants insulated from his evaluation of the similar activities of the group to which he himself belongs.

Precise description of "things" is not in the *Travels* associated with truth. In the linguistic tour de force of the first voyage when the Lilliputian evaluation of the contents of Gulliver's pockets, in particular his watch, is recounted, we see exactitude of description resulting in failure of comprehension (II:34–36). Without a knowledge of the cultural context of these objects, the Lilliputians are misled by the attempted precision of their physical inventory. The later description of Gulliver's hat may at first puzzle even the unwary reader: "a great black Substance lying on the Ground, very oddly shaped, extending its Edges round as wide as his Majesty's Bedchamber, and rising up in the Middle as high as a Man...they had got to the Top, which was flat and even; and, stamping upon it, they found it was hollow within" (p. 41).

The doctrine that words should be as nearly as possible equivalents of things is parodied in the third voyage.[7] The projectors who plan to communicate with a "Bundle of *Things*" make the assumption that "in Reality all things imaginable are but Nouns" (II:185). Their scheme to replace language is based upon a grossly distorted version of mind that is made possible by a very narrow conception of the world. The Struldbruggs,

[7] Irvin Ehrenpreis, "Four of Swift's Sources," *Modern Language Notes* 70 (1955), places the word machine of the third book in the context of anti-Epicureanism (pp. 98–100). Lucretius said that the universe is made of atoms, just as sentences are made of letters. Many readers subsequently turned this analogy against Lucretius's notion of a fortuitously constituted universe, arguing that a universe cannot come into being fortuitously any more than books can. Clive T. Probyn, "Swift and Linguistics: The Context behind Lagado and around the Fourth Voyage," *Neophilologus* 58 (1974), finds a significant number of parallels between Swift's satires of language schemes and the works of John Wilkins (pp. 425–32). Ann Cline Kelly, "After Eden: Gulliver's (Linguistic) Travels," *ELH: A Journal of English Literary History* 45 (1978), 33–54, considers the treatment of language in the *Travels* as Swift's response to various attempts to devise a language that "recaptured the linguistic purity of the Garden of Eden, where words were intimate with the things they represented" (p. 35).

whose language erodes as they lapse into their physicality, are the condition to which these projectors unwittingly aspire.

But the language of the *Travels* that comes closest to conveying so many things in an equal number of words is that of Gulliver in his catalogs of the fourth voyage: "Their next Business is, from Herbs, Minerals, Gums, Oyls, Shells, Salts, Juices, Seaweed, Excrements, Barks of Trees, Serpents, Toads, Frogs, Spiders, dead Mens Flesh and Bones, Birds, Beasts and Fishes, to form a Composition for Smell and Taste the most abominable, nauseous and detestable, that they can possibly contrive, which the Stomach immediately rejects with Loathing: And this they call a *Vomit*" (II:253–54). Many of his descriptions are reduced to lists:

> And, being no Stranger to the Art of War, I gave him a Description of Cannons, Culverines, Muskets, Carabines, Pistols, Bullets, Powder, Swords, Bayonets, Sieges, Retreats, Attacks, Undermines, Countermines, Bombardments, Sea-fights; Ships sunk with a Thousand Men: twenty Thousand killed on each Side; dying Groans, Limbs flying in the Air: Smoak, Noise, Confusion, trampling to Death under Horses Feet: Flight, Pursuit, Victory; Fields strewed with Carcases left for Food to Dogs, and Wolves, and Birds of Prey; Plundering, Stripping, Ravishing, Burning and Destroying. [II:247]

Syntactic complexity implies gradation: it inevitably involves questions of hierarchy—emphasis and subordination. Gulliver verbally reduces European society to an unordered, unconnected heap of foul objects. The connective principle governing his lists is often only the multiplication of evils within a subject area. The list tends to become a number of evils conveyed in an equal number of words.[8] To strip human behavior of its complexities, on the ground that most complexities are invalid social rationalizations for corruption, is a common satiric technique. In the first voyage, Swift reduces the conflict be-

---

[8]W. B. Carnochan, *Confinement and Flight: An Essay on English Literature of the Eighteenth Century* (Berkeley: University of California Press, 1977), traces Gulliver's movement "from fluency to blockage, from speech to speechlessness" (p. 45). The entire discussion is valuable (pp. 45–53).

tween France and England to one that originated in a dispute about the appropriate way to break an egg. He does not allow talk about religion to obscure the drive for domination that motivates the continuing conflict. But this rendering of human activity as if definable in diminished physical terms is susceptible of another interpretation. It may suggest that the very notions of value and spirit are human pretensions without merit.

Indeed, Gulliver's method of definition in the fourth voyage is reminiscent of many of Hobbes's mordant revelations of the concealing linguistic garments on nasty human behavior: for example, "*Honourable* is whatsoever possession, action, or quality, is an argument and signe of Power";[9] "The Value or Worth of a Man, is as of all other things, his Price; that is to say, so much as would be given for the use of his Power" (*Leviathan*, I, 10, p. 151). Behind Hobbes's method of thinking and writing is his premise that all existence is body, although not all language refers to bodies (*Leviathan*, IV, 46, pp. 689–90). The language that Gulliver uses in the fourth voyage to describe European culture eliminates, as Hobbes's definitions do, the metaphysical assumptions that humans use to confer value upon their endeavors. Gulliver's version of an objective account of human civilization reduces it essentially to the destructive use of energy.

The perversions of language among the projectors of the third voyage and Gulliver's satiric idiom of the fourth voyage are Swift's extension of the metaphysical implications of the stylistic program of the Royal Society. Its ideal of language influences Gulliver's style in the first two voyages, is reduced to absurdity in the third voyage, and is turned to satiric uses far from its ostensible purpose in the fourth voyage.

Gulliver's final stance is an attitude that he adopts; it may also be viewed as a way of talking about things. His conversion in Houyhnhnmland is, among other things, a linguistic process. In this voyage Gulliver has the difficult task of translating his world into the Houyhnhnm language, a task that affects his conception of his own culture. He then attempts to

[9]Hobbes, *Leviathan*, ed. C. B. MacPherson (Baltimore: Penguin Books, 1968), I, 10, p. 155.

translate the account for us in the terms by which the Houyhnhnms conceive of it: "My only Concern is, that I shall
hardly be able to do Justice to my Master's Arguments and Ex-
pressions, which must needs suffer by my Want of Capacity, as
well as by a Translation into our barbarous *English*" (II:245).
The Houyhnhnm language, however, as well as the English
language, provides the limits for Gulliver's expression of European culture.[10]

For the Houyhnhnms, the function of language is simple:

> the Use of Speech was to make us understand one another, and
> to receive Information of Facts; now if any one *said the Thing
> which was not*, these Ends were defeated; because I cannot prop-
> erly be said to understand him; and I am so far from receiving
> Information, that he leaves me worse then in Ignorance; for I
> am led to believe a Thing *Black* when it is *White*, and *Short* when
> it is *Long*. [II:240]

They are entirely uninterested in speculation and have not
even any conception of "*Opinion*" (II:267); indeed they disre-
gard much of human intercourse, which is often neither defini-
tively truth nor falsehood. They have no sense of the possibility
that there may be two ways of seeing the same thing, or perhaps more precisely, that there may be *more* than two ways (the
right and the wrong) of seeing something. The notion of the individual, or a subjective dimension, is rejected by them as a diversion from truth: reason "strikes...with immediate
Conviction; as it must needs do where it is not mingled, obscured, or discoloured by Passion and Interest" (II:267). Their
language and thought tolerate abstraction only to a limited ex-
tent: all words to express evils, including a cut foot, are borrowed from the "Deformities or ill Qualities of the *Yahoos*" (p.
275). They tend to conceive of things as sharply opposed exter-

[10]Hugh Kenner, *The Counterfeiters: An Historical Comedy* (Bloomington: Indiana University Press, 1968), alludes to Fortran in describing the Houyhnhnms' language (p. 142). Kathleen M. Swaim, *A Reading of Gulliver's Travels*
(The Hague: Mouton, 1972), finds that "the difficulties of translating words
into and out of the Houyhnhnm tongue make the form of the language into a
several-faceted moral comment" (p. 175).

nalities: black-white, short-long. When Gulliver accepts their viewpoint—their language—he identifies all good with Houyhnhnms, all evil with Yahoo-humans, and adopts as far as possible the physical behavior of horses (galloping and neighing).

Gulliver's accommodation of European civilization to the Houyhnhnm language results in a loss of nuance and an absence of interpretive context. He presents his culture in the physical terms that the European and Houyhnhnm languages have in common and in the polarities characteristic of Houyhnhnm judgment. A lawyer is someone "bred up from. . . Youth in the Art of proving by Words multiplied for the Purpose, that *White* is *Black*, and *Black* is *White*, according as they are paid" (II:248). A soldier is a "*Yahoo* hired to kill in cold Blood as many of his own Species, who have never offended him, as possibly he can" (II:246–47). In these definitions Gulliver strips human disputes of any context, reducing them to what may be called their operational aspects. He removes the dispute from the cultural setting from which it derives its meaning.[11]

The coincidence between the Houyhnhnm language and conventional satiric language allows Gulliver's assertion that his satiric account is literal. But his adoption of a new language is also symptomatic of his loss of a precise sense of identity and the consequent blurring of perspective. The succession of diverse societies in which Gulliver attempts to place himself physically and linguistically culminates in Houyhnhnmland. After Houyhnhnmland only his memory of a past preserved in a book prevents his disintegration, and this book is itself an attempt to distance himself from that past.

The assaults on Gulliver's identity are explicable in the terms of Locke's linguistic and epistemological theory.[12] Ac-

[11]Martin Price, *Swift's Rhetorical Art* (New Haven: Yale University Press, 1953), concludes that Gulliver is finally unable to abstract or to generalize: "Thoroughly literal, he can respond to images but not to their metaphorical significance" (p. 100).

[12]All quotations from Locke are from *An Essay Concerning the Human Understanding*, ed. Peter H. Nidditch (London: Clarendon Press, 1975). Citations are to book, chapter, and paragraph. Swift made a negative comment on Locke's *Essay Concerning the Human Understanding:* "In that there are some

cording to Locke, people, the makers of categories, have an uneasy relationship with their own names: they can be metamorphosed by a word. They want to know whether "a Drill, or a monstrous *Foetus*, be a Man or no," although nature does not distinguish species as we do by our names (III, x, 21). Locke suggests that people take their category from the name that others give them, whatever the ultimate truth about them. Nevertheless a person also has a sense of his own individuality that is not contained by the fiction of an external category and that extends to parts of life that are not open to others. Locke

---

dangerous tenets, as that of *innate Ideas*" (*The Prose Works of Jonathan Swift*, ed. Herbert Davis [Oxford: Basil Blackwell, 1935–68], 97). Kenneth MacLean, *John Locke and English Literature of the Eighteenth Century* (New Haven: Yale University Press, 1936), notes that this remark is a rather temperate one for Swift (pp. 23–24). Furthermore, "among Swift's numerous outbursts against philosophy Locke is spared at least in name and is conspicuously absent from the ranks of the modern bowmen, as the philosophers are called in the *Battle of the Books*" (MacLean, 9). W. B. Carnochan, in *Lemuel Gulliver's Mirror for Man* (Berkeley: University of California Press, 1968), argues cogently that Swift had a strong interest in philosophical issues paralleling those in Locke's *Essay.* He comments that "the *Travels* may be 'Lockean' [only] in a general way" (p. 127) but concludes that the evidence "acquires a cumulative weight" (p. 128). After surveying the attempts to find the influence of Locke in Swift's works, Ricardo Quintana, in *Two Augustans: John Locke, Jonathan Swift* (Madison: University of Wisconsin Press, 1978), concludes that "Swift had read Locke and was quite aware of his commanding presence in the Augustan intellectual scene" but that "it is not clear that he ever borrowed from him significantly, and he certainly never made him an unmistakable object of his satire" (Quintana, 81). I am not convinced by Quintana's assertion that "Swift as a traditional philosophical realist dismissed Lockean empiricism with impatience" (p. 76). Swift's belief that the rejection of innate ideas was "dangerous" and his irritation with Tindall for writing of the *idea* of something rather than of the thing itself (Quintana, 77) do not constitute an unequivocal attack on Locke's epistemology. Furthermore, Locke's epistemology is not precisely a rejection of philosophical realism. Locke finds that people are unable to perceive essences; nevertheless, he does not deny the existence of essences. He attacks those who are "so sceptical, as to distrust...Senses, and to affirm, that all we see and hear, feel and taste, think and do, during our whole Being, is but the series and deluding appearances of a long Dream, whereof there is no reality" (IV, xi, 8). In Locke's view, our "assurance of the Existence of Things without us, is sufficient to direct us in the attaining the Good and avoiding the Evil, which is caused by them, which is the important concernment we have of being made acquainted with them" (IV, xi, 8).

took up such issues when he added a discussion of personal identity to the second edition of his *Essay* (1692).

Locke differentiates "identity of man" (external) from "identity of person" (internal). The identity of man consists in a "participation of the same continued Life, by constantly fleeting Particles of Matter, in succession vitally united to the same organized Body" (II, xxvii, 6). This kind of identity is external and physical, enabling us to recognize others by their observable characteristics.[13] "Personal identity," however, is a matter not at all of the body but of memory. Locke makes a distinction between the external categorization by others and the subjective sense of self. A *"Person...* can consider it self as it self, the same thinking thing in different times and places; which it does only by that consciousness, which is inseparable from thinking....as far as this consciousness can be extended backwards to any past Action, or Thought, so far reaches the Identity of that *Person"* (II, xxvii, 9). One "person" may have several different bodies or several persons may be connected to the same body: "It being the same consciousness that makes Man be himself to himself, *personal Identity* depends on that only, whether it be annexed only to one individual Substance, or can be continued in a succession of several Substances" (II, xxvii, 10). Here Locke defines the implicit situation of metamorphosis—a sustained consciousness and a changing form. This understanding of Locke's definition is apparent in the discussion of personal identity printed in *The Spectator* (No. 578, August 9, 1714), which was conducted by means of a story about a king who entered a deer and, finally, his queen's lap-

---

[13]One of Locke's examples concerns a talking parrot that gave evidence of rationality. Despite the parrot's abilities, concludes Locke, men think of it as a parrot, not as a man (II, xxvii, 8). Irvin Ehrenpreis, "The Meaning of Gulliver's Last Voyage," in *Swift*, ed. Ernest Tuveson (Englewood Cliffs: Prentice-Hall, 1964), an article reprinted from *Review of English Literature* 3 (1962), 18–38, notes that Locke had taken his anecdote of a talking parrot from Temple's *Memoirs*, which Swift had prepared for the press: "To Swift the story would have been peculiarly familiar, since...Swift...made the copy of the *Memoirs* which was sent to the printer" (*Swift*, ed. Tuveson, 132). Ehrenpreis comments on Locke's extensive discussions of conventional definitions of species, definitions that Locke regarded as arbitrary and imprecise.

dog but maintained the same personal identity throughout his physical changes. Personal identity is in Locke something that people recognize (or construct) for themselves: the identity of man is something given to one. Personal identity must be understood (or created) by the introspection of a self-conscious being.

Gulliver's travels result in a series of metamorphoses that are related to the problems of identity implied by Locke's discussion. Like Apuleius's ass, Gulliver sees and is seen in a different way because of his altered positions in society. The metamorphoses of Gulliver, however, result from the hardened and limited conventions of his perceivers, not from a magical transformation of his body. In the second voyage he passes through a bewildering series of transformations (some minor but others extreme) in the eyes of his human and animal beholders: weasel, clown, baby, clockwork, monkey, tortoise. In the first two voyages his major transformations are to giant and dwarf, still versions of the human, but in the fourth voyage he becomes an animal, a smart one, but nevertheless of the Yahoo species. Although Gulliver is not himself apparently metamorphosed in the third voyage, both the Laputans and Struldbruggs of that book are partial transformations of the human form.

The second and fourth voyages, especially, show the process of Gulliver's losing and attempting to regain a precise and appropriate sense of self. He is physically disoriented by the Brobdingnagians and the Houyhnhnms, and he internalizes their alien modes of perception. Although he undergoes a process of reorientation after these voyages, the effects accumulate, as the ending of the fourth voyage shows. Human failure to understand the essences of natural creatures is as marked in the *Travels* as in Locke, and Gulliver's changing situations illustrate the Lockean distinctions between the identities of persons and of man. The sharp discrepancies between these two kinds of identity lead to Gulliver's final condition.

The King of Brobdingnag believes Gulliver to be clockwork (II:103) but changes his mind because of the reason evident in Gulliver's language. Nevertheless, as Gulliver painfully senses, the King continues to place him in the category of an animal: "He was strongly convinced to get me a Woman of my own Size, by whom I might propagate the Breed: but I think I should rather have died than undergone the Disgrace of leaving a Posterity to be kept in cages like tame Canary Birds" (II:139). The giants find it difficult to give Gulliver the identity of man because they differ physically from him, but Gulliver has a sense of personal identity that links him to the human more tightly than any physical characteristics could.

In the fourth voyage the Houyhnhnms too recognize Gulliver's rudiments of reason but think that he primarily needs more animal defenses—longer nails, tougher skin (II:242–43). Gulliver too responds to his perception, not of essences, but of Houyhnhnm physical characteristics: his moral enlightenment is accompanied by an imitation of the Houyhnhnms' neighing and galloping. Yahoos seem to have the identity of man but not, in Locke's words, the "reason and reflection" of a "thinking intelligent Being," which is what "*Person* stands for" (Locke, II, xxvii, 9). The creatures who have a consciousness resembling, although superior to, Gulliver's have the identity of horses. In Lockean terms, the "persons" are horses and the "men" are Yahoos. Faced with the irreconcilable separation in fact that Locke acknowledges hypothetically, Gulliver makes an attempt to become a horse, to bring his outer form into conformity with that of the creatures whose consciousnesses seem most to resemble his own.[14]

In *The Gaping Pig: Literature and Metamorphosis,* Irving Massey argues that metamorphosis entails the separation of private

[14]R. S. Crane, "The Houyhnhnms, the Yahoos, and the History of Ideas," in *Reason and the Imagination, 1600–1800,* ed. J. A. Mazzeo (New York: Columbia University Press, 1962), pp. 231–53, shows that, in making man irrational and the horses rational, Swift reverses the conventions of the logic texts of his time. While persuaded of the importance of this background, I an uneasy with Crane's assertion that "it will doubtless be agreed that one question is kept uppermost in [the fourth voyage] from the beginning, for both Gulliver and the reader . . . : what sort of animal man, as a species, really is" (p. 243). I do not find (except perhaps in a very loose sense) the "central issue" to be "primarily one of definition: is man, or is he not, correctly defined as a 'rational creature'?" (Crane, 243). Like Locke, Swift is eroding this unanswerable question of an abstract definition of man, rather than asking it again.

from public language.[15] In his view, Lucius's metamorphosis in *The Golden Ass* severs him from public language, a restriction that becomes a source of increased understanding: he "will never come to understand life as long as he participates in the exchange of ignorance that passes for human communication; in his silent existence as ass he can begin to know the limits of knowledge, the realities of experience, and glimpse the contours of the fate that suits him" (p. 26). Massey conceives of our public speech as "external, non-personal": "In dream we speak our own language, when we wake the language of others" (p. 30).

This dichotomy between the private and the public is a major theme in Locke: in Rosalie Colie's words, "Descartes and Hobbes had made the assumption that ideas are formed from sense-experience, and were concerned with the adequacy or inadequacy of ideas thus formed; Locke examined something even more individuated—the inner life of ideas thus formed."[16] Locke's conception of the function of language is that of mediating between this inner world and a public one.

Locke defines language as a system of signs of internal conceptions (III, i, 2), which, nevertheless, has an important social function: "God having designed Man for a sociable Creature" gave him "Language, which was to be the great Instrument, and common Tye of Society" (III, i, 1). Because we can conceive only of "outward sensible Perceptions, or of the inward Operations" of our minds, we draw words from the areas of more easily shared sensible perceptions in order to make pri-

[15]Irving Massey, *The Gaping Pig: Literature and Metamorphosis* (Berkeley: University of California Press, 1976), 78.

[16]Rosalie Colie, "John Locke and the Publication of the Private," *Philological Quarterly* 45 (1966), 34. Ronald Paulson, *The Fictions of Satire* (Baltimore: Johns Hopkins University Press, 1967), cites the view of Ernest Tuveson, in *The Imagination as a Means of Grace* (Berkeley: University of California Press, 1960), 26, that the Lockean epistemology influenced literature "toward contemplation of the world as seen by the mind rather than on 'truth' per se" (Paulson, 150-51). Paulson concludes that "though Swift disagreed with the doctrine of the *Tabula rasa*, he found in every other way a philosophy of mind suited to his satiric mission of attacking the reason that claimed too much for itself or that deceived itself" (p. 150).

vate experience socially available (III, i, 5). Locke's description of this "Tye of Society" implies that it defines neither the external nor the internal with exactitude. Instead, the demand for social intercourse creates in language a compromised structure that corresponds neither to that of nature nor to that of the self. This warping of the private into the more conventional and public is regarded by Massey as an implicit theme of fictions of metamorphosis. The only escape from the bifurcation of public and private is, in Massey's view, that achieved by the artist, who "is the only one who contends successfully with the demand for public and private speech at once, who can say something to others without having had to relinquish his state of dream" (p. 31).

Gulliver is Swift's version of the artist who must link public and private speech. But as might be expected, in the *Travels* the private eventually masquerades as, and subverts, the public. This process begins with an intolerable suppression of the private but ends with the "author's" creation of a fictional world that serves his needs. When Gulliver enters a strange country, a public language is demanded of him, and the language that he knows becomes private, a silencing of at least some aspects of his identity. This silencing of the private accompanies his metamorphoses within the societies of his various hosts, as essential aspects of his humanity escape them. The language experiments of the Academy of Projectors provide a thematic replication of this relationship between language and metamorphosis. The attempt to make language entirely public metamorphoses language itself; language becomes a silent bag of objects as unlinguistic as Lucius the ass. Such a language may be manipulated by human beings, but, embodying nothing of them, it performs none of the functions of self-definition or mediation. And without their language, humans, like the Struldbruggs, are metamorphosed into alien creatures.

The Houyhnhnms conceive of language as public, a device "to receive Information of Facts" (ii:240). The public and private, however, meet easily for them because the structures of their minds and those of their society reach a near identity. But in learning their language, Gulliver is required to relinquish much of himself. Nevertheless, he also recovers many of the aspects of his culture through his discussions with his Houyhnhnm master. He instructs the Houyhnhnm in European vices by means of "Similitudes" (II:243), creating a *translatio* for his humanity, vicious as it is. This communication of his own culture is a source of satisfaction to Gulliver: "But being of an excellent Understanding, much improved by Contemplation and Converse, he [the Houyhnhnm] at last arrived at a competent Knowledge of what human Nature in our Parts of the World is capable to perform" (II:244). Gulliver, like one version of the critic in *A Tale of a Tub*, is pleased to be dabbling in the excrement that is Swift's symbol for egocentricity. Gulliver's language here performs a mediating function, both that of distancing himself from mankind and that of bringing the Houyhnhnm closer: the Houyhnhnm acquires a "Disturbance in his Mind" and fears that "his Ears being used to such abominable Words, might by Degrees admit them with less Detestation" (II:248).

Gulliver's supreme fiction is that he speaks with objectivity, that he uses the Houyhnhnm language of fact. But this public language expresses a private need. Because his experience is of violent change, Gulliver attempts to impose the fixity of apparently universal truths. He establishes his identity as author, as mediator between Houyhnhnms and people, using his fiction-making capabilities to assimilate the public to the private. His continuing attempts to describe his worlds with extraordinary precision and concreteness are in part defenses against the consequences of the metamorphoses that deprive him even of the security conferred by a stable linguistic category.

In summary, the suppression of subjectivity that is apparent in the Royal Society's attitude toward observation is used by Gulliver as a way of suppressing his complicity in human experience. Discussing the style of certain Royal Society reports, Ronald Paulson remarks, "Two living personalities are communicated to us: the poor creature itself, and the conductor of the experiment, remaining aloof, cold and unfeeling."[17] In the

[17]Ronald Paulson, *Theme and Structure in Swift's "Tale of a Tub"* (New Haven: Yale University Press, 1960), 57.

Travels, Gulliver himself is both creature and experimenter, both callous subject and quivering object, distancing his former self as well as contemporary humanity.[18] Locke's *Essay* explores the problems in this sharp separation of subject from object, as Locke considers both our perceptions of self and of others. Locke describes the frailty of the identity claimed by people, based as it is on an unstable linguistic category and on a fallible memory. Like Locke, Swift shows the difficulties of finding a privileged position from which to describe a society and a self that bear a constantly changing relationship to each other. Gulliver's linguistic program for resolving or exploiting the separation of subject from object is no more fixed, no less mutable, than its world or its user.

[18]Robert C. Elliott, "Gulliver as Literary Artist," *ELH: A Journal of English Literary History* 19 (1952), 40–62, studies the double point of view in the *Travels.*

CHAPTER 7

Epistemological Foundations

"'Empiricism' is derived from the Greek word for 'experience,'" remarks A. D. Nuttall, but "it is the great irony of English empiricism that, through reverence for a scientific metaphysic, it soon proved hostile to experience."[1] Empiricism's sharp differentiation of subject from object, observer from observed, threatens to erect an insurmountable barrier between self and other. Although a conventional function of reason is to interpret information from the senses appropriately, the development of empirical science imposes the intermediaries of experimentation and instrumentation between the senses and reason. Furthermore, the doctrine of primary and secondary qualities resolves experiential assumptions about the external world into an inventory of those qualities that are part of external reality and those that are only in the subject's perceptual apparatus.

Scientific empiricism subjects the rough and ready version of Baconian empiricism found in Swift's *Tale of a Tub* to considerable stress. Reason and the senses had there been conceived as counterweights that limited, but nevertheless rectified, each other. But if the information of the senses is not merely limited but also seriously unreliable, people are of necessity Peters and Jacks, banging into posts with closed eyes and unable to justify

[1] A. D. Nuttall, *A Common Sky: Philosophy and the Literary Imagination* (Berkeley: University of California Press, 1974), 20.

a distinction between bread and mutton. Nuttall defines the solipsistic tendency of British empiricism by an illustration of a boy, standing for the mind or soul, who sits in the upper windowless room of the house that is the body: "He has never been out of his cell. All he knows of that distant, grey spire, those feathery trees, has been mediated to him" by a "bizarre apparatus" of "nerve wires" (p. 13).

The epistemological issues in empiricism are germane to the *Travels,* as they were to the *Tale of a Tub.* The third voyage of the *Travels* takes up the new science more explicitly than any other work of Swift's and ends by implying an even less optimistic view of the potentialities of reason and sense than did the *Tale of a Tub.* The same negative epistemology is apparent: separating reason from sense, mind from body, is madness. But in the *Travels,* the conjunction of reason and sense results in an apparent constriction, not in a seemingly sensible moderation. Swift's *Travels* shares the Royal Society's suspicion of human subjectivity but not the Society's optimism about overcoming it.

The temptations to solipsism are very powerfully represented in Swift's satires. The tale-teller seeks to retreat into the house of fiction, and Gulliver retreats to a stable, collecting around himself the smells and shapes that will stimulate his memory of a past existence and will suppress the anguish of his real condition. Swift's examples of a satisfactory adjustment of reason and sense, the internal and the external, to each other are few and undeveloped as compared with his powerful examples of the distortions of reason. The preponderance of attack is, of course, the feature that categorizes his works as satire; nevertheless, a generic classification is not appropriately used if it defines as unnoteworthy those qualities in the work that rub against an a priori category. Swift's unwillingness to enclose his satiric works within the boundaries set by the absolute judgments of an olympian satirist makes the aberrations of his creatures expand beyond their allotted functions. The notion that the reader should consider only the attack of satire, without pondering its limits and the nature of the values that engender the attack, is derived from the assumption that the attack itself is definitive. In this view, it is assumed that the exposed evils

are such because the satirist and the reader notice their repul-
siveness. But this version of satire is undermined when the satirist is drawn into the scene but is not precisely separated from
the author (as in the *Travels,* when the very authorial choices
that create the scene for us are dramatized). The reader's belief
in a posited integrity of the satirist enables him to consider only
the satirist's attack, but this attack is itself drawn into the satiric scene when the authorial privilege is questioned. Swift's
rendering of his satiric figures' rush into a self-created world
makes questionable the assumption that these figures are aberrations; they may represent a human condition that is inevitable even if recognized and defined. In Swift's satires, the
satirist's depiction of a sick world does not make him immune.
Nor can the reader acquire superiority merely by acquiescing
in the ready-made vision of the "author."[2]

The possibilities of reason are explored in the third and
fourth voyages of the *Travels,* primarily through a contrast of
Laputans and Houyhnhnms. The flying island and its men
with one eye turned inward and the other upward are images of
the separation of reason from experience. This version of reason is abstract and speculative, consulting only the self and its
ambitions. The Houyhnhnms, horses, exemplify a reason
wholly allied to nature. Their reason is relatively incurious and
is linked so securely to their experiences that they are frequently in error about the greater world beyond them.[3] Swift

[2]While I am in general agreement with Robert C. Elliott, "Swift's Satire:
Rules of the Game," *ELH: A Journal of English Literary History* 41 (1974),
413–28, which argues that "the satirical attacks on satire of both [Wyndham]
Lewis and Swift are launched from higher levels than their object," I am not
willing to accept without qualification Elliott's conclusion that "according to
the rules of the game the position of the authors is privileged" (p. 427).
Swift's satire makes us at least question the rules of the game by which an author is privileged.

[3]James E. Gill, "Beast over Man: Theriophilic Paradox in Gulliver's Voyage to the Country of the Houyhnhnms," *Studies in Philology* 67 (1970), 532–49,
examines the "inversion of human and animal traits" in the fourth voyage,
pointing out the paradox that Houyhnhnm reason is both "more inclusive"
and "more restricted" than man's (p. 548). C. J. Rawson, *Gulliver and the
Gentle Reader: Studies in Swift and Our Time* (London: Routledge and Kegan
Paul, 1973), 23–25, examines the multiple meanings of nature and reason in
the *Travels,* concluding that "Swift's concern is not to boil the issue down to

Epistemological Foundations

appears to be limiting their reason to the construction of an ethical system relevant to their world alone. Houyhnhnm reason is an ideal condition of a limited faculty.

In allowing Houyhnhnm reason to encompass matters of conduct but not the supernatural, Swift is rebuking not the Houyhnhnms but physicotheology, which had long lauded the study of nature as the cure for atheism. Human conduct, Swift's fable suggests, is far inferior to that which these horses achieve by their reason without divine revelation, yet people continue to admire human reason, regarding it as an adequate tool for comprehending the divine despite its failure even to order a just society.[4]

By means of the invidious comparison of perverse Laputan reason to this limited, although excellent, Houyhnhnm reason, Swift again attacks the rationalism that he had earlier satirized. The Laputans, although ignorant of practical matters, will give their judgments in "Matters of State" unhesitatingly, Gulliver remarking that he had "observed the same Disposition among most of the Mathematicians I have known in *Europe*" (II:164). Later, in Glubbdubdrib, Gulliver hears Aristotle make the same invidious contrast between the rational and the empirical. Aristotle relegates "Systems of Nature" to "Fashions":

---

its commonplace propositional content, but to exploit the damaging ironies by all the verbal means which the language puts at his disposal" (p. 25).

[4]Kathleen Williams, *Jonathan Swift and the Age of Compromise* (Lawrence: University of Kansas Press, 1958), 187–92, and Martin Kallich, *The Other End of the Egg* (Bridgeport: Conference on British Studies at the University of Bridgeport, 1970), 74–84, argue that, because the Houyhnhnms represent "the dream of the Deist and the rationalist" (Williams, 187), they must be objects of Swift's satire. The arguments of both Williams and Kallich expose the difficulties of asserting that the Houyhnhnms are examples of Swift's ideals, against which all else is to be measured. Nevertheless, the argument that the Houyhnhnms are objects of satire is tortured. In my view, Swift is satirizing people to whom Christianity has been revealed for not being able to live up to "the dream of the Deist and the rationalist." Some of the difficulties in analyzing the fourth voyage are obviated if reason and nature are not regarded as opposed to revealed religion. Although for Swift reason and nature are insufficient, they are not inimical to revealed religion. See Phillip Harth, *Swift and Anglican Rationalism: The Religious Background of "A Tale of a Tub"* (Chicago: University of Chicago Press, 1961), chap. 2.

"Even those who pretend to demonstrate them from Mathematical Principles, would flourish but a short Period of Time, and be out of Vogue when that was determined" (p. 198). Acknowledging "his own Mistakes in Natural Philosophy," Aristotle attributes them to his having in many things to proceed "upon Conjecture, as all Men must do" (p. 197).

Aristotle includes in his critique the theories of two natural philosophers already attacked in Swift's writings—those of Descartes and Gassendi—and goes on to include another theory, "*Attraction,* whereof the present Learned are such zealous Asserters" (II:197–98). As Margaret C. Jacob has shown, the latitudinarians of the late seventeenth century used Newton's "natural philosophy and the new science in general as a counterweight to what they called the atheism of the Hobbists, Epicureans, and radical freethinkers."[5] Swift, however, dispenses with the help of Newton's theory, lumping it with the Cartesianism that it had superseded and with the Epicureanism of Gassendi. In his *Tale of a Tub,* Swift had promulgated versions of Aristotle, Descartes, Hobbes, and Bacon that were generally accepted in the late seventeenth century. In addition he had rather ingeniously linked Descartes, Hobbes, and Gassendi in ways that showed similarities of thought or effect that underlay their obvious differences. But when Swift includes Newton in his satire, he attacks a figure thought by many of his contemporaries to be a mainstay of Christianity, in contrast to Hobbes and Descartes.

Newton's writings imply a universe that may decay, and Swift's mockery of Newtonianism links it to the schemes of millenarians like Burnet (earlier satirized by Swift), who (from Swift's perspective) combined an arrogant belief in the ability of human reason to comprehend the divine plan with a ludicrous obsession with the earth's degeneration. In the *Opticks,* for example, Newton says that there must be some active principle of motion in the world or "the Bodies of the Earth, Planets, Sun, and all things in them, would grow cold and freeze, and become inactive Masses; and all Putrefaction, Gen-

[5]Margaret C. Jacob, *The Newtonians and the English Revolution, 1689–1720* (Ithaca: Cornell University Press, 1976), 19.

eration, Vegetation and Life would cease, and the Planets and Comets would not remain in their Orbs."[6] Comets are a force for an irregularity, which "will be apt to increase until this system wants a reformation" (*Opticks*, p. 402). Margaret Jacob believes that Edmund Halley "quite probably spoke for Newton" when he read a paper to the Royal Society describing the catastrophic effects of a collision between the earth and a large body such as a comet (Jacob, pp. 135–36). The Laputans' "continual Disquietudes..., Their Apprehensions...from several Changes they dread in the Celestial Bodies" (II:164), are derisively applicable to Newtonianism.[7]

These Laputan visions of cosmic disaster are generally similar to those that are evoked in Lucretius and are studied by the millenarian Burnet. A comparison of Newton to Lucretius (or to his master Epicurus) was not unprecedented, having already been made admiringly by Halley. J. R. Albury shows that Halley's "Ode" of forty-eight lines prefacing the first edition of Newton's *Principia* was modeled on portions of Lucretius's *De rerum natura*.[8] In the "Ode" Newton is praised in ways reminiscent of Lucretius's praise of Epicurus (Albury, pp. 28–31). A staunch disciple of Newton, Halley had in 1691 been charged with "asserting the eternity of the world," and he was consequently rejected for the Savilian Chair of Astronomy at Oxford. Bentley, another of Newton's champions, revised

---

[6]Isaac Newton, *Opticks* (New York: Dover, 1952), 399–400. See Jacob, *The Newtonians and the English Revolution, 1689–1720*, 135–36, and David Kubrin, "Newton and the Cyclical Cosmos: Providence and the Mechanical Philosophy," *Journal of the History of Ideas* 28 (1967), 325–46, for discussions of this aspect of Newton.

[7]David Renaker, "Swift's Laputians as a Caricature of the Cartesians," *PMLA* 94 (1979), 936–44, argues that the "Laputians' fear of the extinction of the sun" is a "a satire on Cartesian cosmology" (p. 940). I find this element of the book to be relevant to Newtonianism; nevertheless, I agree with Renaker's contention that Laputa exemplifies general aspects of Cartesianism. Swift conflated Newtonianism with the Cartesian rationalism that it replaced. Renaker's remark that Descartes is not mentioned in Sprat's *History* (p. 940) is, however, erroneous (cf. Sprat, *History of the Royal Society*, ed. Jackson I. Cope and Harold Whitmore Jones, Washington University Studies [St. Louis: Washington University, 1958], 95–96).

[8]J. R. Albury, "Halley's Ode on the *Principia* of Newton and the Epicurean Revival in England," *Journal of the History of Ideas* 39 (1978), 24–43.

Halley's "Ode" for the 1713 edition of the *Principia* (the one listed in the sale catalog of Swift's library) and removed some of the offending passages.

The Struldbrugg episode is an attack on the arrogance of linking the scientific and the moral as the physico-theologians (Newtonians and others such as Burnet) did, making man's moral condition depend heavily on his intellectual achievements. In his vision of immortality, Gulliver expects to "see the Discovery of the *Longitude,* the *perpetual Motion,* the *universal Medicine,*" and to make "wonderful Discoveries" in astronomy "by observing the Progress and Returns of Comets, with the Changes of Motion in the Sun, Moon and Stars" (ii:210). Gulliver believes too that longer life would bring progress in morality. The "Observations and Memorials" of men who live forever would give "perpetual Warning and Instruction to Mankind: which, added to the strong Influence of our own [the Struldbruggs'] Example, would probably prevent that continual Degeneracy of human Nature, so justly complained of in all Ages" (ii:210). He grafts a theory of progress onto a myth of decline, revealing the arrogance that may lurk in the most melancholy versions of the decay of nature. Although the Struldbruggs may appear to support some notion of nature's decline, the oldest are worst, not best (ii:214). In contrast to the Struldbruggs, the Houyhnhnms are able to die at about age seventy, when their physical and their mental powers too diminish (ii:275). Both groups suggest the individual physical and mental limitations of organic life.

Any discussion of eighteenth-century epistemology is of necessity closely related to the philosophy of language. The sharp separation of object from subject makes prominent the question of the reality to which language corresponds—is it that of the subject, the object, or only its own? Both Hobbes and Locke agree that all our conceptions originate in physical experiences (*Leviathan,* I, i, p. 85; *Essay on Human Understanding,* II, i, 24) but also recognize that external physical reality is not the content of the mind.[9] Ernst Cassirer defines the resultant con-

---

[9]Hobbes, *Leviathan,* ed. C. B. MacPherson (Baltimore: Penguin, 1968); *An*

flict in the empiricists' thoughts about language: "The more sharply they defined language not as an expression of things but as an expression of *concepts*, the more imperiously the question was bound to arise as to whether the new spiritual medium here recognized did not falsify rather than designate the ultimate 'real' elements of being. From Bacon to Hobbes and Locke we can progressively follow the development and increasing acuteness of this question, until at last in Berkeley it stands before us in full clarity."[10]

Swift replicates the intellectual failures that he represents elsewhere in the *Travels* in his treatment of language in the third voyage. One process of misconception is materialistic— connecting language to physical reality—and leads through a "computation" of the parts of speech in books (II:183-84), to a rejection of all but nouns, and finally to an end in a series of objects that are undifferentiated from the nonlinguistic world (II:185). The other process of misconception is rationalistic—the exaltation of language to a meaning in the user's mind but freed from correspondence to any external reality, as when the Laputans describe the beauty of their ignored women in the terms of their obsessions—mathematics and music (II:163). Gulliver ends his narrative of the Academy of Projectors with a summary illustration of the semiotics implied by these two views of language: a projector describes a way to discover plots by examining excrement, and Gulliver describes a way to discover them by allegory and anagram (II:191-92).

The projector who compiles books from the arbitrary collocations of phrases on a moving frame assumes a third position—that language is itself something, not merely a transparency: he "had emptied the whole vocabulary into his Frame, and made the strictest computation of the general Proportion there is in Books between the Numbers of Particles, Nouns, and Verbs, and other Parts of Speech" (II:184). This

Essay Concerning the Human Understanding, ed. Peter H. Nidditch (London: Clarendon Press, 1975).

[10]Ernst Cassirer, *The Philosophy of Symbolic Forms*, trans. Ralph Manheim (New Haven: Yale University Press, 1953), 1:136.

language is intended to correspond to the language of other books, not to the world or to a person. Swift's implication here as elsewhere is that any valid epistemology requires a connection between subject and object and that language itself should convey such a connection. But the epistemological and hermeneutical problem that Swift has raised remains: Is language not a system in itself that exists without any necessarily adequate correlation to subject or object? Is language itself not an analyzable thing like excrement or planetary motion?

Michel Foucault's analysis of the assumptions that made the achievements of the seventeenth- and eighteenth-century thinkers possible—the "classical episteme"—is useful for placing Swift's treatment of the subject of language in an epistemological context that is broader than the expressed philosophy of language of the thinkers that Swift satirizes or exemplifies.[11] The intense concern with language reform and with universal grammar in Swift's time is part of a larger group of assumptions about the human understanding.

Foucault remarks, "The existence of language in the classical age is both pre-eminent and unobtrusive" (p. 79). It is pre-eminent because it represents thought and unobtrusive because all aspects of it other than this representation are effaced. Foucault contrasts the classical view of signs to the Renaissance view, using as the basis for comparison the classical conception of "representation" as opposed to the Renaissance conception of "resemblance." In the Renaissance a sign was a thing among other things, needing to be discovered through its resemblance to whatever it is the sign of. But the sign of the classical age "has no content... other than what it represents" (p. 64) and is "constituted only by an act of knowing" (p. 64). Classical language withdraws from things and becomes neutral (p. 56), but the Renaissance episteme allows "nature and the word [to] intertwine with one another to infinity, forming, for those who can read it, one vast single text" (p. 34).

In the classical age language has a special function not allotted to other signs. It represents representations, making it pos-

[11]Michel Foucault, *The Order of Things: An Archaeology of the Human Sciences* [*Les mots et les choses*] (New York: Random House, 1970).

sible to analyze thought itself (p. 83). Having the function "of providing adequate signs for all representations, whatever they may be, and of establishing possible links between them," language can recall representations and perform operations on them (pp. 85, 82). Classical language is then "discourse," a "sequence of verbal signs" that makes it possible to analyze and reorder the "simultaneity of representations" (p. 83).

But Foucault discerns a contradiction—a *"point of heresy"*— in this view of language. Eighteenth-century grammar divides language between "discourse" and "designation," discourse emphasizing the articulation of a "whole network of complex relations (succession, subordination, consequence)" (p. 99), and designation emphasizing "the obscure nominal function that was thought to be concealed in those words, in those syllables, in those inflections, in those letters that the over-generalized analysis of the proposition was allowing to pass through its net" (p. 101). The linking of language to knowledge led eventually "towards the place where things and words are conjoined in their common essence, and which makes it possible to give them a name" (p. 117). This tendency of classical language to find its culmination in a name is finally a reassertion of language "in its brute being" (p. 119), a rejection of discourse. In the interest of clarity it may be useful to summarize Foucault's complex point even more baldly (perhaps even crudely). The classical episteme assigned language the function of representing our understanding of something. Such a representation presents itself as discourse, an analysis conducted according to appropriate categories of thought and measurement. But the more completely discourse fulfills this function, the more nearly it approaches its object. Ultimately, complete understanding is embodied in the perfect name. But language has then become a thing itself, not only a representation: it becomes a thing equivalent to things, much as in the Renaissance episteme.

In relation to Foucault's analysis, Swift's satirical image of words becoming objects is somewhat more elusive than it first appears to be. The image may imply that the projectors have returned to the former kind of thinking—the Renaissance episteme—in which case the word-objects are returned to nature and must be interpreted as one among other elements of nature. On the other hand, the image may suggest derisively the fallacy of any belief in a conclusive representation, a complete conceptualization of something. If complete conceptualization were possible, discourse would then no longer be necessary, only this representation. The image of language as a bundle of things may be a depiction of the end (in both senses) of discourse, in which language reaches a condition of "brute being."

These two versions of language are similar: in both, language, having achieved being, loses its transparency. There is also a difference. When returned to a place in the book of nature, language is subject to commentary, the never-ending attempt "to uncover the great enigmatic statement that lies hidden beneath...signs" (Foucault, pp. 80–81). But the "brute being" that language achieves through a total conceptualization, a final naming, can be interrogated only through criticism, an analysis of a name's "truth, precision, appropriateness, or expressive form" (p. 80). Discourse is then restored by our uncovering of the process by which the true name was acquired.

Swift's mockery of words dissolved (or crystallized) into things is directed against the belief in the possibility of a final conceptualization of things. His criticism recovers the process of such presumed conceptualization and shows it to be one of suppression rather than of increasing understanding. The language experiments of Lagado inexorably suppress the elements of discourse until only a nominating function is left. The bookmaking machine is an attempt to produce autonomous discourse; however, only portions of its output can be salvaged by a human being, who is needed to identify the discourse elements. Subsequent projectors resolve that anomaly by retaining only the nominating function of language, which is capable of being carried in single words or in portions of words.

Swift's rejection of the presumption of possible exhaustiveness in the conceptualization of things is easily confused with a very different attitude—the rejection of language as a representation and, consequently, as a means of analysis. The reason for the confusion is that Swift's method for satirizing the belief in the possibility of a complete conceptualization of the natural world is to ridicule it by linking it to the earlier view that language is only one thing among other things of nature. Paracelsus, among others, regarded the world as populated by signs, with everything a sign of something else, a view that Swift associates with the aberrations that he attacks in the *Tale*. When Swift shows language ending in wooden models, he denotes inadequate conceptualization, and he also connotes an atavistic return to language that escapes conceptualization and becomes part of the flux of things.

Foucault points out the evident conflict in "classical rationalism": "The forces of nature and life refusing to let themselves be reduced either to algebra or dynamics, and thus preserving, in the depths of classicism itself, the natural resources of the non-rationalizable" (pp. 56–57). Swift's assertion of the forces of nature and life is to be construed not as an abandonment of the classical view of language and analysis but only as an assertion of the limits of reason when it is confronted by nature. The Struldbruggs are Swift's most powerful image of an atavistic contradiction to ever-increasing conceptualization. Gulliver envisions extended life as bringing solution after solution to intellectual problems, but instead it brings a return to life that is merely organic. Without memory, the Struldbruggs are also without language, and without language they are without thought. Written language provides a continuity that overcomes time and space, but this continuity is subverted by organic collapse. The Struldbruggs are an extreme version of a condition that prevails among the Laputans, who are without "Imagination, Fancy, and Invention . . . , being shut up within Mathematicks and Music" (II, 165–66). Their election of these two sciences to which to subordinate nature is a deliberate constriction that parallels in effect the organic collapse of the Struldbruggs. Swift's mockery of the Laputans, however, is not a rejection of all analysis. The imagination that the Laputans lack is necessary for the comparisons and differentiations essential to analysis. The Laputans lack the imagination and the Struldbruggs the language that are necessary for the kind of analytic operations that Foucault finds to be characteristic of eighteenth-century thought.

A curiosity of eighteenth-century thought is that its science and its skepticism advance together. Foucault explains this feature as a result of its system of signs, especially "taxinomia," the science of identities and differences of beings. When forced to deal with nonsimultaneous things, "taxinomia" must define "the general law of beings, and at the same time the conditions under which it is possible to know them": "Hence the fact that the theory of signs in the classical period was able to support simultaneously both a science with a dogmatic approach, which purported to be a knowledge of nature itself, and a philosophy of representation which, in the course of time, became more and more nominalist and more and more skeptical" (p. 74). Swift exhibits this skeptical attitude toward representation without rejecting a science of order. The Houyhnhnms are an assertion of order even while their understanding of that order (in Foucault's terminology, their "representations") falls short of reality. Swift implies the ultimate inadequacy of our rationalizations of nature without rejecting the system of signs as the source of whatever knowledge we can acquire. Houyhnhnm thought is ludicrous only insofar as Gulliver attempts to turn it into a kind of analysis and a language that is adequate to all reality.

Foucault states, "In the classical period, what was denoted by the term universal language was not the primitive, pure, and unimpaired speech that would be able . . . to restore the understanding that reigned before Babel. . . . The universal language does not restore the order of days gone by: it invents signs, a syntax, and a grammar, in which all conceivable order must find its place" (p. 89). Many philosophers of language, among them Wilkins and Sprat, referred to some prelapsarian ideal of language, but their aim was to produce a "sign system that linked all knowledge to a language, and sought to replace all languages with a system of artificial symbols and operations of a logical nature" (p. 63). The attempt to find the primitive true language is, according to Foucault's analysis, linked to the

Renaissance episteme: "these insistent marks [of language] summoned up a secondary language—that of commentary, exegesis, erudition—in order to stir the language that lay dormant within them and to make it speak at last" (p. 79). In contrast, the classical episteme effaces this notion of an ur-text: "One no longer attempts to uncover the great enigmatic statement that lies hidden beneath its signs; one asks how it functions: what representations it designates, what elements it cuts out and removes, how it analyzes and composes, what play of substitutions enables it to accomplish its role of representation. *Commentary* has yielded to *Criticism*" (pp. 79–80).

In *A Tale of a Tub*, Swift parodies commentary, allowing the will to escape discourse, each word, syllable, and letter carrying an independently definable meaning. Commentary and digression merge and swell, displacing the text. The tale-teller intends his language to be not nomination, the classical period's conceptualization of things, but a sign among other signs, as vast as the book of nature. He exploits the metaphoric relationships between the thing that is language and other things, for example, language is weighty or light, our thoughts rise or fall, and our books sink or swim. Language is part of the great web of resemblances, the word "ears" linked to hearing, to readers, and to private parts.

In the *Travels*, Gulliver's intention is contrary, his language aiming at an increasingly complete conceptualization, the univocal naming that implies finality of understanding. This goal is achieved by the Houyhnhnms: they exhibit the "perfect transparency of representations to the signs by which they are ordered" that Foucault sees as the limits of the knowledge that is bound by the classical episteme (p. 76). The Houyhnhnms' language defines what is, in the terms of Houyhnhnm representations—black and white, long and short, Houyhnhnm and Yahoo. Their language is not a definition of the variousness of the world and the complications of its resemblances with the aim of grasping some obscured meaning, but an ordering of the world according to their methods of measurement.

Swift's implications about language and the limits of conceptualization are similar to those of Locke, whose thinking is governed by some of the variants of the classical episteme that Foucault describes. Both Swift and Locke respond to a sense of the incommensurability of the human understanding and the organic world by emphasizing discourse rather than designation, the relation of language to mental operations rather than to ideas of physical things. According to Murray Cohen's analysis, "communication, for Locke (and Arnauld), is not the mere exchange of words that are the names of ideas, but more importantly the demonstration of a mental 'action...relating to those ideas' (Locke's *Essay* 3.7.1). The words that connect the names of 'things' (nouns, pronouns, adjectives, and verbs) are particles that relate not only 'the parts of propositions, but whole sentences one to another, with their several relations and dependencies, to make a coherent discourse.' "[12] Cohen finds that Locke participates in an intellectual change in which "the philosophical basis of language moves from the nature of external reality to the structure of the human mind" (p. 55), a movement that results in a grammar emphasizing substantives less and a "syntax of connectives" more (p. 60). For Locke, conceptual identity between a word and the totality of a natural thing is not possible. When Adam named "jealousy" and "adultery," he put together ideas in his own mind, but when he named "gold," the thing he named extended beyond all his capacities for understanding it (III, vi, 46).

For Locke, the categories of language do not make possible an analysis of substance but often only conceal our failures of understanding. In order to think and talk, we sort things into "Species," an "Artifice of the Understanding," which erroneously appears "to preserve those *Essences,* and give them their lasting duration" (III, v, 9–10). Furthermore, these failures of language are not corrected by science but are concomitant with its limits: "In the Knowledge of bodies, we must be content to glean, what we can, from particular Experiments: since we cannot from a Discovery of their real Essences, grasp at a time whole Sheaves: and in bundles, comprehend the Nature and

---

[12]Murray Cohen, *Sensible Words: Linguistic Practice in England, 1640–1785* (Baltimore: Johns Hopkins University Press, 1977), 40, 41.

Properties of whole Species together" (IV, xii, 12). Because we can reach little "general Knowledge" about bodies, Locke suspects "that natural Philosophy is not capable of being made a Science" (IV, xii, 10). He insists, however, that he does not "dis-esteem or *dissuade the Study of Nature*" (IV, xii, 12). Although he "readily" agrees that contemplating God's works leads to an admiration of their "Author" (IV, xii, 12), his eye, like that of the King of Brobdingnag, is on the practical. He rebukes the tendency of people to demand a rational certainty that exceeds the limits of their understanding: "He, that, in the ordinary Affairs of Life, would admit of nothing but direct plain Demonstration, would be sure of nothing, in this World, but of perishing quickly" (IV, xi, 10).[13]

In a description similar to Swift's later account of Houyhnhnm conceptualization, Locke defines the basis of all our knowledge as "intuition":

> Thus the Mind perceives, That *White* is not *Black,* That a *Circle* is not a *Triangle,* That *Three* are more than *Two,* and equal to one *and Two.* Such kinds of Truths, the Mind perceives at the first sight of the *Ideas* together, by bare *Intuition,* without the intervention of any other *Idea;* and this kind of knowledge is the clearest, and most certain, that human Frailty is capable of. This part of Knowledge is irresistible, and like the bright Sun-shine, forces it self immediately to be perceived, as soon as ever the Mind turns its view that way; and leaves no room for Hesitation, Doubt, or Examination, but the Mind is presently filled with the clear

[13]David A. Givner, "Scientific Preconceptions in Locke's Philosophy of Language," *Journal of the History of Ideas* 23 (1962), states that Locke "did not understand the logic, procedure, and goal of the new mathematical physics. When he asserted that a science of substances could not advance beyond furnishing an imperfect catalogue of their properties, that the nature of bodies could not be comprehended under universal principles, and that the mathematical method was not applicable to a science of substances, he thereby denied the very things that Galileo and Newton had dramatically achieved" (p. 349). I cannot accept Ricardo Quintana's sharp separation of Locke and Swift on the basis of their attitudes to science (*Two Augustans: John Locke, Jonathan Swift* [Madison: University of Wisconsin Press, 1978], 130–31). Unlike Quintana, I do not find that Swift looks upon all science as misdirected intellectual energy, nor do I find that Locke rejects the belief that man's moral being is more important than his scientific knowledge.

Light of it. It is on this *Intuition,* that depends all the Certainty and Evidence of all our Knowledge. [IV, ii, 1]

Houyhnhnm reason, however, confines itself to the certainty of intuition only by disregarding much that human beings think important. Locke recognizes that human beings must often depend on "demonstrative knowledge," achieved by a process "which we call *Reasoning*" (IV, ii, 2). Such reasoning is based on intuitions but results when a series of ideas is put together to show a relationship between two ideas whose agreement is not immediately apparent. He then adds to intuitive and demonstrative knowledge our *sensitive knowledge* "of the existence of particular external Objects" (IV, ii, 14). This kind of knowledge is more than "bare probability" but does not attain the degrees of certainty that mark intuitive and demonstrative knowledge. Much that we assume to be certain, Locke says, is only a matter of probability: "It becomes the Modesty of Philosophy, not to pronounce Magisterially, where we want that Evidence that can produce Knowledge. . . , for the state we are at present in, not being that of Vision, we must, in many Things, content our selves with Faith and Probability" (IV, iii, 6).

Robert Martin Adams defines the situation of Swift and his generation as follows: "Generally speaking, the seventeenth century fell into psychology as into an ambush. Locke's experience summarized in capsule form that of the entire century. Setting out to dispute a substantive matter, he and his friends quickly found themselves at a complete stand, unable to determine anything until they had come to an agreement concerning human understanding and the degree of certainty to which it could properly aspire. Swift fell into the same pit and never succeeded in getting out of it, perhaps because he never wanted to."[14] *A Tale of a Tub* and the *Travels* initiate a process of regression in which each perspective is revealed to be only a portion of a larger one, allowing no possibility for finality. The *Tale* assesses the consequences of the separation of mind from body,

---

[14]Robert Martin Adams, *Strains of Discord: Studies in Literary Openness* (Ithaca: Cornell University Press, 1958), 161.

implying that any such separation is a rationalism needing to be disciplined by the empirical. This empiricism, however, promises little but a temporary correction of a previous position. The *Travels* analyzes empiricism, showing that it too can become the substance of a fiction as undisciplined by reality as the tale-teller's deliberate rejection of nature. Compared with Hooker's vision of an ordered world that is discernible by human reason and may include human institutions, Swift's vision in his major satires is a retreat from the human, although not from nature, reason, or God. As Swift remarks in one of his sermons, "*Reason* itself is true and just, but the Reason of every particular Man is weak and wavering, perpetually swayed and turned by his Interests, his Passions, and his Vices" (9:166). Human disciplines fail to rectify these evident failures of reason, and even the artist is able only to record the advent of the chaos and night that extinguish clearly discernible light. Swift's choice of the "Author" as his encapsulating fiction asserts the power and responsibility of the subject—the perceiver and creator—even as this view of the subject is shown to be anomalous. The subject's inevitable desires for preeminence drive him to impose and expose the defects of his private visions. Swift uses this compromised authorial figure as his central symbol both of the limits of the human understanding and of the seemingly limitless human capacity for constructing fictions that make private perversions appear to be public institutions.

But it is from this capacity for constructing fictions that the literary energy of Swift's satires derives. The opacities of the wall separating subject from object inspire not silence but ingenious language. From the perceived failures of human reason, Swift and his "author"-narrators construct narratives that appear to traverse time and space, taking us with them on their pilgrimage which, we learn gradually, does not result in progress. Nevertheless, when their, and our, fictions are exposed, we then arrive not at the austere security of bare literal truth (which is nothing without a fiction to comprehend it) but at more inclusive fictions. Swift, in a sense, deplores this repetitiousness. Still, he also invests with enormous interest the whirling and vertiginous movement through the mighty maze that we eventually discover is self and whose convoluted paths are mapped by an "author" of doubtful authority.

Ignoring the reluctance of Swift, eighteenth-century fiction embraced the narrative program that he analyzed in the *Travels,* seizing the literal as its validated medium but covertly manipulating the seemingly public truth in the interest of the fascinations of private revelation. Formal realism presumes that an achieved literal has justifiable claims to be unmediated truth: authors are suspect (even if they are autobiographers), but the added validation of witnesses, dates, details, and documents is a corrective. But Michael Seidel's remark concerning certain kinds of satire also applies to novels that make similar claims: "To insist that what any intelligent reader perceives as a fictional construct is indeed an historical record is to make the very issue of authority or 'legitimacy' part of the fictional subject at hand."[15] Novelistic fiction immediately begins that inextricable intertwining of public and private that leads eventually to the plausible assertion that character and event are indistinguishable in novels. Think of Sterne. And even in Defoe, whose novels were written between *A Tale of a Tub* and the *Travels,* the apparent circumstantiality is no more its own reward and validation than is the circumstantiality of the *Travels.* As John Richetti remarks, "To a degree, the facts...with which Defoe's characters present themselves are converted by the process of narration into emanations of the self and proof of its power."[16]

Edward Said's view of the novelistic tradition as growing from "the desire to create an alternative world, to modify or augment the real world through the act of writing,"[17] accords with Swift's analysis of the liabilities of fiction and its makers. Both *A Tale of a Tub* and the *Travels into Several Remote Nations of the*

[15]Michael Seidel, *Satiric Inheritance: Rabelais to Sterne* (Princeton: Princeton University Press, 1979), 61.

[16]John Richetti, *Defoe's Narratives: Situations and Structures* (Oxford: Clarendon Press, 1975), 19.

[17]Edward Said, *Beginnings: Intention and Method* (New York: Basic Books, 1975), 81.

World depict "authors" who create a fictional alternative to a perceived world that is insufficient. From Swift's point of view the consequences are in both cases a form of madness; they also illustrate two different, although related, approaches to fiction. The *Tale* progressively discovers itself as an attempt to suppress the world, the *Travels* as an attempt to supplant it. Although the tale-teller seemingly relegates language to the status of other natural objects, he does so not to equate language with the natural world but to subordinate the natural world to his language. Conversely, Gulliver insists on the analytical exactitude of his language but ends by giving his allegiance to the words themselves. In both works the "author"-narrators are explicitly implicated in their fictional constructions, but the tale-teller's implication in his fiction becomes identification with it, while in the *Travels* Gulliver's fictional construction is eventually accepted by him as a world more objective and consistent than the one in which his readers live. Gulliver's fiction consequently insulates him from the complexities of his world, while the tale-teller and his fiction collapse simultaneously.

These two analyses of fiction making are related to (although not necessarily derived from) those issues in *Don Quixote* that have led readers to find in that work the stream-head of the novel. The insistence on everyday experiential criteria for the ambiguities of reality (the Sancho Panza view of life) is less likely to be strikingly disconfirmed than is the attempt to impose an already disconfirmed fiction (in Don Quixote's case, the romance) on reality. Nevertheless, as *Don Quixote* shows, any conception of reality is inevitably shaped by fictional categories, and Sancho Panza, like Don Quixote, is a maker of fictions. The novel that subsequently develops makes an implicit but striking claim that fiction making is one of the more important activities of the human mind, but this subsequent tradition of the novel often chooses also to claim that it is a valid version of external reality. The ingenuities of fictional elaboration that are used to conceal and to reveal a self while making claims of public truth are to Swift examples of the perhaps inevitable poverty of the human understanding, and they are the stock in trade of the subsequent tradition of fiction.

Index

Steele, Peter, 119
Sterne, Lawrence, 11-12, 51-52
Stout, Gardner, 68-69
Swaim, Kathleen, 150
Swift, Jonathan: *Argument Against Abolishing Christianity*, 31-32; *The Battle of the Books*, 88-90, 92, 94; *A Discourse Concerning the Mechanical Operation of the Spirit*, 59, 88-90, 96-100; *The Drapier's Letters*, 24; *A Modest Proposal*, 69; *Mr. Collins's Discourse of Free-Thinking Put into Plain English By Way of Abstract, for the Use of the Poor*, 45; *The Sentiments of a Church of England Man*, 30; *Sermons*, 177

Temple, Sir William, 92-94, 99, 102, 105-106
Thomas Aquinas, Saint, 28-29, 43-46

Traugott, John, 31
Travel literature, 25, 113-16, 123, 135-40
Tuveson, Ernest, 99, 156

Uphaus, Robert W., 28
Utopia, 114-15, 123-35, 138

Vickers, Brian, 91, 124

Wasserman, Earl, 29
Watt, Ian, 15
Webster, Clarence M., 35
Wedel, T. O., 128-29
White, Hayden, 17
Wilkins, John, 172
Williams, Harold, 43
Williams, Kathleen, 52, 132-33, 163
Wotton, William, 63, 84-85, 93, 101, 105-108

Library of Congress Cataloging in Publication Data

Zimmerman, Everett.
  Swift's narrative satires.

  Includes index.
  1. Swift, Jonathan, 1667-1745—Criticism and interpretation. 2. Satire,
English—History and criticism. 3. Swift, Jonathan, 1667-1745. Tale of
a tub. 4. Swift, Jonathan, 1667-1745. Gulliver's travels. 5. Narration
(Rhetoric) I. Title.
PR3728.S2Z55   1983   823'.5   83-45176
ISBN 0-8014-1595-0